Puffin Books
Editor : Kaye Webb

'On the skirts of the moor' or 'on the edge of the beyond' people said when they talked about Sunset Farm, and to young Peter Varden who lived at Sunset Farm the words had held a special fascination. There was his home, so familiar, safe and hardworking, and only just beyond it the vast, treacherous tract of Dartmoor, so bleak and threatening in winter or enveloped in one of its sudden and bewildering mists.

Peter's own great singlehanded struggle with Dartmoor came when he was still a little boy. It was haymaking time, a boiling hot day 'with a temperature', as Peter's sister Beth put it. Anyone could see that it was going to rain, and the best hay would be ruined unless the entire family worked like demons to get it in.

So it was that Peter was sent alone for the very first time to fetch the cows home for milking, and when he couldn't find them he went looking on the open, dangerous moor. Here, instead of a sunset there seemed to be something evil and threatening, and Peter could see nothing. No tors, no skyline, no cows, nothing. He was lost in a grey swirling, Dartmoor fog.

For readers of eight and over.

Cover design by Hans Helweg

To Sunset and Beyond

Alec Lea

Puffin Books
in association with Hamish Hamilton

Puffin Books: a Division of Penguin Books Ltd,
Harmondsworth, Middlesex, England
Penguin Books Australia Ltd, Ringwood,
Victoria, Australia
Penguin Books Canada Ltd, 41 Steelcase Road West,
Markham, Ontario, Canada
Penguin Books (N.Z.) Ltd, 182–190 Wairau Road,
Auckland 10, New Zealand

First published by Hamish Hamilton 1970
Published in Puffin Books 1973
Reprinted 1974

Made and printed in Great Britain by
Hazell Watson & Viney Ltd
Aylesbury, Bucks
Set in Linotype Pilgrim

Dedicated to Judith and Kenneth

The idea for this book came from a grave-stone, a real grave-stone, that stands in a prominent place in the churchyard of Walkhampton, a village on the western outskirts of Dartmoor. The inscription on the stone runs as follows:

In memory of George Grey, died July 20, 1843, aged 8 years who being placed in charge of some horses lost his way in a fog on Dartmoor and after wandering for two days was found in a state of exhaustion and died soon afterwards.

Contents

1 Sunrise at Sunset 9
2 Breakfast at Sunset 19
3 Miss Scrimshaw 26
4 Late for Haymaking 34
5 Carrying Hay at Sunset 44
6 Going for the Cows 55
7 In the Jaws of the Fog 66
8 Where's Peter? 74
9 Beth at the Moor-gate 80
10 Gone to Earth 89
11 Dreaming 95
12 Wet Morning 105
13 Nearly Found 114
14 River Music 119
15 The Cavalcade 128
16 Sunset at Sunset Farm 132

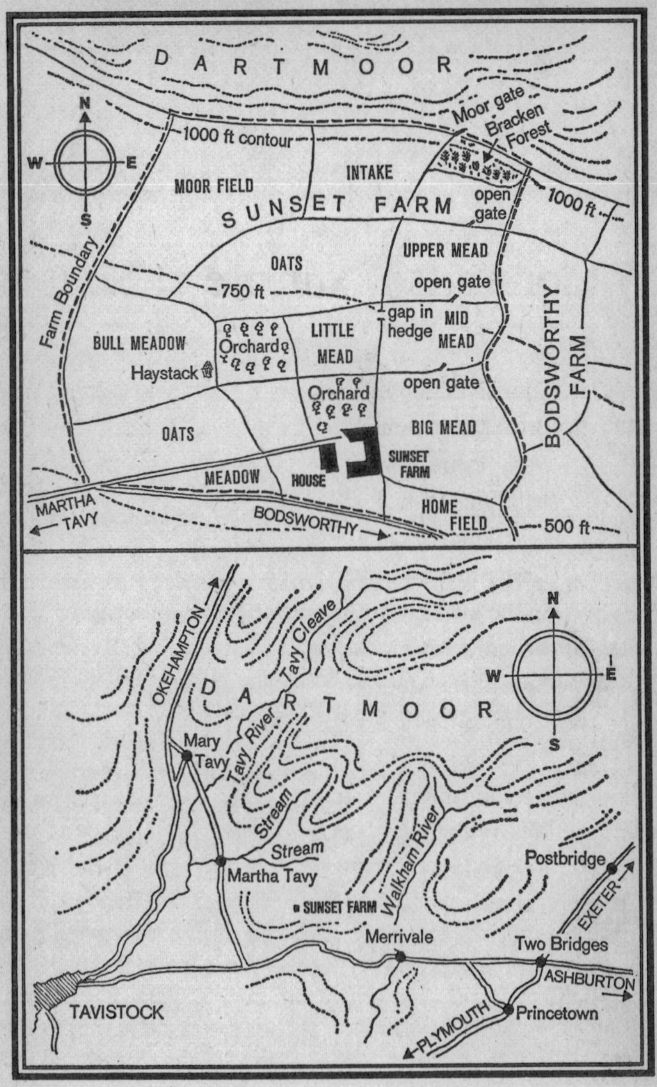

DARTMOOR
Moor gate
Bracken
Forest
1000 ft contour
INTAKE
MOOR FIELD
SUNSET FARM
open
gate
1000 ft
UPPER MEAD
OATS
Farm Boundary
open gate
750 ft
gap in
hedge
MID
MEAD
BODSWORTHY
FARM
LITTLE
MEAD
BULL MEADOW
Orchard
Haystack
open gate
Orchard
OATS
BIG MEAD
SUNSET
FARM
MEADOW
HOUSE
HOME
FIELD
MARTHA
TAVY
BODSWORTHY
500 ft
OKEHAMPTON
Tavy Cleave
DARTMOOR
Tavy River
Mary
Tavy
Stream
Walkham River
Stream
Martha Tavy
Postbridge
SUNSET FARM
EXETER
Merrivale
Two Bridges
ASHBURTON
TAVISTOCK
PLYMOUTH
Princetown

1. Sunrise at Sunset

As I sit here alone in my Dartmoor cottage, staring into the fire and hearing the wind howling over the moors outside, I look back down the long years at those three children on their moorland farm at the end of the last century. Night after night I conjure them out of my memory and watch them, rooted as they were in that simple earthy stay-at-home life they used to live, in the days when a galloping horse was the fastest thing that moved and everyone went to bed by candle-light. One of those three children was lucky. He was given a special day that stretched and widened him, a day that made it possible for him later on to have the whole world for his home, insead of that one little pocket of Devonshire land.

I ought to know what that one day did, because I was the boy. In fact I still am, because I can remember everything that happened that day, every single little detail from its very beginning until its very end. Although how can one say exactly when a day as extraordinary as that really came to an end? Was it when the last trickle of daylight finally leaked out of the sky? Oh no, it went on long after that, it went on even after the black night of fear and dreams was over and a new day was dawning for everyone else, but not for me because I was still so far away in a world of my own.

For what is it really that ends one day and starts another? It is getting into a bed at night and getting out of it in the morning. On my longest day I never went to bed at all, so when another morning came it was for me the same day just going on.

It wasn't the longest day of the year, because it was July 21st not June 21st. But it was *my* longest day. Not only the longest day I had had in my life up to that time but also the longest I have had up to *this* time, and I am old enough now to have grandchildren. So when I want to know what my grandchildren are thinking and feeling all I have to do is to live again my special unforgettable summer day long ago, the one that began with Granma's voice at twenty minutes to five in the morning and ended – well, let me tell you the story and then you can decide for yourself when it ended.

The three of us were Sam, Beth and Peter, and we were Vardens of Sunset Farm. Sam was the eldest and I, Peter, was the youngest. All the early part of that summer I had been so proud of being a Varden, because I had made a little discovery of my own about what Vardens and their farm were really like. It happened this way.

On Easter Sunday all seven of us from Sunset Farm went to church. It was a special occasion, and we all went in the pony-trap, Pa and Ma, Granma and Granpa, and we three children. It was four miles each way, up and down great hills, and on most of the uphill parts we had to walk to rest the horse, that is all except Granpa who was short of breath because he was forever smoking his pipe. The other special occasions for church were Christmas Day and Harvest Festival, but very often the weather was so bad at Christmas that we couldn't go at all. There's no way of keeping dry in a pony-trap. Granma used to say it was rightly called a trap because it held you there defenceless in the teeth of pouring rain and buffeting wind.

Well, on that Easter Day Beth and I and Sam were playing hide and seek in the churchyard, letting off steam after a service that had gone on for nearly two hours. The grown-ups were all gossiping round the church door or on the path leading down to the gate and some of them had even spilled out among the graves, because the church had been full to overflowing. I was hiding behind a tombstone and there were two men talking nearby. Suddenly I pricked my ears up when one said to the other –

'Oh ay, 'course I knaws the Vardens. Everyone knaws the Vardens o' Zunzet – proper varmers they be an' all, up there to Zunzet.'

And the other man said – 'Ay, an' so they need to be, for 'tis very hard going, 'way up there on the very skirts o' the moor.'

That was how I made my discovery about what Vardens were and what Sunset Farm was. The skirts of the moor, the man said, and for a moment I saw our great old Dartmoor as a very huge mysterious cloudy queen sitting high up on lots of different kinds of rocky thrones and looking out over the green fields of Devon. The skirts our farm sat on were her western skirts facing out towards Tavistock and Brentor and leading your eyes far away into the sunsets over the Cornish moors. Our house was long and low, with a thatched roof and with nearly all its windows looking west. That was why it was called Sunset. No one ever looked out of our windows in the evenings without noticing what the sun was doing, whether it was going down in glory or in misery. It used to make so much difference, especially to Granma, because she was a member of the family who had special knowledge about the weather. When I look back to those days now, it seems to me that Granma claimed to have special knowledge about almost everything. But Ma and Pa never did. They just knew things without making a fuss about it.

My longest day began with Granma's voice. It was the kind of voice you remember for a life-time. It had a peculiar way of cutting the air, like a knife going through a big hunk of cheese. It wasn't very loud, but it pierced things easily, not only by its sound but also by what it said. It always went straight to the point in any situation, in fact there was something *inexorable* about it, I mean that it belonged with all those things you would avoid altogether if you could, but you know you can't because they are part of the very stuff life is made of – like crying, for instance, or dying, or sitting indoors with rain beating all day against the windows, or hearing a pig or a hen getting killed outside in the yard.

So Granma's voice rang through the house on my longest day, all those years ago. She must have been standing on the stairs where she could see two things – a patch of the eastern sky through the staircase window, which looked out on the back side of the house, and the barometer hanging on the wall so as to be at eye-level with anyone who halted half way up or down.

'God bless my soul, the sun's up and out and there's not a body stirring in this house!'

Vibrant and indignant the voice was, with the firm intention of driving all sleep out of the house in the shortest possible time. But there was also a note of anxiety in it that morning, which gave it even more piercing power than usual.

It happened very often that it was Granma who wakened

the household and really it was a most useful thing for her to do. In those days there were no cheap alarm clocks to be had and in haymaking time it was very important to get up really early because every bit of daylight was precious. So as a matter of course we had all been getting up about sunrise for weeks and because it had been a hot dry summer we were all rather over-tired and short of sleep, especially we three children. On wet days we were allowed to lie in bed till eight and get a really good rest, but in that third week of July there had been no wet days for an awful long time.

After Granma's voice there was a sound of creaking beds all over the upstairs of the house. I was sitting up in bed looking at Sam, who was awake too but making a face meaning that he didn't want to get up. Then Pa's voice came, very deep and a bit slow as it always was –

'All right, Mother doant 'ee fret thysel, 'tis only a quarter before five.'

Half-past four had been our very latest time for getting up all through that summer so far, for the sun rose at the proper time in those days, before the Government started messing about with the clock. That morning it rose at four-twenty. Our biggest and best field of hay was nearly ready to bring in, so it was by far the busiest time of the whole year. If the long spell of fine weather hadn't made us all a bit lazy and easygoing we would have been up at four that morning.

Pa's voice didn't smooth Granma down much. It seldom did, though it tried to do so about fifty times every day.

'God bless my soul,' said Granma again, from the same place on the stairs. That got me out of bed, and Sam too, and we could hear Beth getting out of hers in the room next door. We never much liked it when God blessed Granma's soul, in fact we strongly wished he wouldn't because it nearly always meant that something was going wrong. So we nipped out of bed mighty quick when her soul got blessed twice over in the first few minutes of the day. This was a warning to all three of us that we were in for some really troublous things. I think it was at that moment that I had my first strange feeling that the day that was starting was going to lead to some very exciting and perhaps even rather terrible things.

Ma and Pa must have got the warning too. Ma put her head in at our door and said, rather snappily for her –

'Now then, you two, downstairs and be quick about it,' as if we couldn't even be allowed time to dress.

Pa must have thrown his clothes on in no time, because he had joined Granma on the stairs. After her second 'God bless my soul' she had called out to him –

'Son, do 'ee come quick and look at this,' and when I poked my head out of our room half-dressed I saw her and Pa taking a good look at the barometer. Pa was shaking his head and saying 'fallen steep – fallen steep it has and no mistake' and then Granma said – 'Didn't I tell 'ee wind was backin' south last night?' Pa caught sight of me watching and shouted out –

'Come on now, Beth and Peter, get you both out after those cows this minute. We'll be havin' streams o' rain by evenin'. And there'll be no school today.'

For me, that was the first thing that went wrong, that day. No school – that meant no drawing, because it was a Thursday, which was the special morning for that. Drawing was my favourite subject, the one thing I was really good at, in fact I was the best one in the school. Drawing was like a sort of magic for me in those days and the mistress used to give me special tuition and make a fuss of me. Missing school did not matter to us children at all, during haymaking time we took it for granted that we would miss as many days as we went. But missing a Thursday, that meant an awful lot to me. It was a disaster, because it would be such a long time before Thursday morning came round again. Besides, I had done some very special drawings at home since last week and the mistress would be wanting to see them. She only came on Thursdays and she was a real artist and she told me I could be a real artist too if I worked at home. One of my drawings was a picture of Beth, done in coloured crayons. It was very special indeed, my first real work of art. All the family were very taken with it, though Granma said it made her look like an angel and that there weren't really any children like that. But she didn't know Beth as I did.

Beth came out of her room, still fastening up her dress, fixed her great big eyes on my face and said softly, 'Oh, Peter!' It was all she needed to say. She was a most extraordinary girl because she always knew what you were feeling and, what was more, she always *cared* about what you were feeling, in fact she really seemed to care as much about your feelings as about her own. She had great wide-apart brown eyes but the strange thing was many people thought she had blue ones. The reason was that the white part of her eyes, I mean the eyeball itself, had a clear bluish tint. Sam and I both had blue eyes.

She and I ran downstairs together (we did everything together except sleep in the same room and we would have liked to do that too) and as we went I heard Ma say to Pa in their bedroom –

''Tis a Thursday, John – Peter'll break his heart if he can't get to his drawing.'

I couldn't hear Pa's reply, but I didn't need to. He was not the sort of man to change his mind. He never had a lot to say, but what he did say he usually stuck to.

Beth and I went to the dairy first to drink a mugful of milk, as we always did, then into the back kitchen to put on our boots and then straight out through the yards to fetch the cows in from the fields. This was always our first job, but Sam had a different one. He had to get the kitchen fire ready for lighting, then pump the day's supply of water from the well, then be ready to go out with Pa to get in the horses. That was how our family used to divide up for the day's work. Ma and Beth and I were in charge of the cows and the calves and the poultry. Pa and Sam were in charge of the horses and the sheep and the pigs, Granma and Granpa looked after the house and the dairy work. It was going everywhere with Pa that made Sam feel so superior to us. Beth and I were always together, but he was always on his own with Pa. Pa never said that his work was more important than ours, but that's what Sam always claimed. He had got it into his head that cows and milking were women's work and Beth and I used to struggle to get it out of his head again. Ma helped us in this all she could.

'Coo, isn't it hot already,' Beth said as we toiled up across the first field. Most of the fields at Sunset were behind the house and sloped steeply up towards the moors. The sun was as scorching as midday and the grass was bone-dry. Every morning for ages now we had got our boots wet and cool with the dew – but not this morning. Everything was different this morning.

The ten cows and the bull when we reached them at the top of the second field were all standing watching us, instead of busily grazing wet grass as they usually did in the cool of the morning, and when we got behind them to drive them down towards the yards they suddenly kicked up their heels and took off at a run as if they were highly delighted about something. Beth and I were left there looking down across an empty field, except for dear old Brindle, the oldest and gentlest cow in the herd, who was stiff in one leg and would never run any more.

So we had time to stay for a minute and realize what a very shining morning it was. From that field if you looked westwards you could see all the very green low country beyond Tavistock, with little villages and churches half hidden by big trees and with roads and rivers winding away into a far distance of quietness and sunshine. And if you looked the other way there was that great mysterious thing called Dartmoor, long slopes of heather and bracken leading up higher and higher to the tors, those castles of grey granite that were so often hidden in mist and cloud in the early mornings. But they were not hidden this morning. With the sun behind them they were all standing out as clear as crystal, seeming much nearer than usual, rather as if they were taking a good look at Beth and me.

And they made us feel so small.

Beth's eyes met mine. 'Isn't it going to be a funny day, Peter?' she said gravely. I distinctly remember that she said 'funny' though she didn't mean funny at all. She just couldn't think of the better words, like peculiar or queer.

'Oh, so you feel it too,' I said quickly, which was silly of me because I must have known that she always felt everything I felt.

'And the cows do, too,' she said. ''Tis like a day with a temperature. It feels to me just a *little* like it did that time I was ill and the doctor came every day and Mum kept taking my temperature all the time.'

She had had quite a bad illness in the early spring and we had all been worried about her. I think it was tonsilitis or something like that.

'But I don't mean I'm ill *now*,' she assured me when she

saw how closely I was looking at her. 'I'll race you to the shippen if you like.'

We started off together and ran like the wind, quite forgetting poor old Brindle, but that didn't matter because we knew she would never stay up there all by herself. We caught up with the cows just as the first one was entering the yard and saw Ma opening the shippen door for them.

'They know there's rain coming, that's what's livened 'em up so,' she called out to us.

Cows always love wet weather in summer because it gives them freedom from flies for a little while and makes their grass taste nicer and grow quicker.

'Keep back out of the way now, you two,' Ma called again sharply, knowing there might be a scrimmage of cows round the doorway because they were all so excited.

And there *was* a scrimmage. It was just the sort of thing that was sure to happen on 'a day with a temperature'. The bull mounted one of the cows just as she was entering the shippen and tried to go in with his front legs on her back. His massive head went full tilt into the wooden beam over the doorway. There was a terrific crack and some of the wood splintered. The poor bull was knocked silly for a moment and as soon as he found his legs again he shied off into the yard and stood shaking his head and blinking his eyes. We watched Ma to see whether we ought to laugh or cry.

She looked at him hard and then smiled.

'Well, that'll teach him a lesson,' she said. 'Let him bide out there and cool down.'

We were half way through the milking before he came slinking quietly into his usual stall as if he hoped no one was looking.

2. Breakfast at Sunset

Milk pouring into a bucket straight out of a cow's teats makes a very soothing noise, especially when you milk fast and there is an inch of froth all over the top of the milk. It sounds rather like a kettle on the boil just ready to make tea with, or like a big cat purring by the fire, only it's much louder than either of those. And the smell that comes up out of the bucket and sinks right into you through your nose and mouth – so sweet, so warm, so safe – that is something I can never forget.

Beth and I were always given the easier cows to do while Ma did all the rough ones, which was really rather hard luck on her, because there's such a big difference between an easy cow and a tough one. For instance, even Beth and I with our small hands could get half a bucketful of milk in five minutes out of Daisy or Buttercup. But Brindle, with her great old thick teats like parsnips – well we just couldn't milk her at all and even Ma took about twenty minutes over it and finished up with the sweat running into her eyes.

That morning Ma wanted us to milk fast to make up for being late, so I knew she wouldn't be very pleased when I started to talk. But on my third cow I had gone back to thinking of school and of my drawings that were all ready to take to Miss Scrimshaw, the drawing mistress, who wasn't really a mistress at all but an artist, because she didn't get paid anything for coming to teach one morning each week. Suddenly I was struck by such a horrible thought that I had to call out at once to Ma, who was three cows away.

'Ma, when is it school term ends?'

She replied that it was some time next week, either Wednesday or Thursday, she thought.

'Oh,' I said in a despairing tone. 'Oh, then – that means Miss Scrimshaw won't come any more, after this morning. Oh, Ma –'

I must have started crying then, because Beth, after leaning out from her cow to snatch a look at my face, called out –

'He's crying, Ma. And it's his silent kind.'

I usually cried without making a sound. It was something I had carefully practised. It worked better than Beth's system, which she also had developed into a fine art. She used to open her mouth very wide and make as much noise as possible, so that it just had to be stopped at once, because it fairly yelled and throbbed unbearably inside your ears and inside your brain. So grown-ups always had to do *something* for Beth, to stop her, even if it wasn't what she really wanted. But with me, since very often no one knew I was crying, or how long I had been at it, there was no point in doing anything for me except the one thing I wanted. Besides, there were some people, Pa for instance, who seemed to take silent crying more seriously than noisy. Ma didn't though. I think she knew that I could turn it on or off when I wanted, and that Beth couldn't. As for Sam, he had given up crying and had begun to swear instead, except when there were grown-ups about.

Ma didn't say anything, so Beth leaned out from her cow again and whispered –

'Peter, perhaps it'll start raining in time for us to go after all.'

I had already thought of that and rejected it as hopeless because the sun was streaming blindingly into the shippen. Besides it was wicked to hope for rain with all that lovely hay lying out there in Bull Meadow nearly fit to carry. Pa would be cross for days if that got spoiled and when he was cross the whole farm went wrong like sour milk.

'That's wicked,' I whispered back, deciding to stop crying now that Ma knew I had been doing it.

'But I'm not *wishing* it,' Beth said. 'I'm only saying it.'

When Ma got up from her cow and walked past me towards the dairy she said –

'You can stop crying, Peter. I've got an idea. I'll write a letter to Miss Scrimshaw and then maybe you can go and see her in the holidays.'

Ma was like that. She used to get lots of ideas and they usually began with writing letters, which she was very good at because she had worked in an office in Tavistock before she married Pa. She wrote Pa's business letters for him.

So by breakfast-time I was fairly happy again, though I know that both Beth and I were a bit weighed down by thoughts of all the hard work that was waiting for us afterwards. With the sun so hot already and no dew and the glass falling steeply, Pa would want us out turning the hay just as soon as we'd finished eating.

We two and Ma were already at table eating porridge (Granma and Granpa always had their breakfast earlier) when through the open windows and door of our big kitchen we saw Sam come racing across the yard from the stables calling 'Hooray' as if it was his birthday or something, while Pa followed him at a sober walk. From the sink in the back kitchen, where he stopped to wash his hands, he announced triumphantly –

'I'm takin' Jack to Blacksmith.'

When he came beaming to the table I said, rather grudgingly I'm sure –

'Oo, you *lucky* thing!'

But Ma said, 'Oh dear.'

Pa came in a moment later, saying to Ma – 'He's cast a shoe – isn't that a plaguey piece of ill-luck to start a day like this with?'

But we could tell he wasn't badly put out, for if he had been Sam would never have dared to show such glee. Jack was one of our two big farm horses, our best horse really because he was quiet and a bit slow, which meant that children could handle him safely. Our other big horse, Jill, who was his sister, was what was called 'scarey' – a very fast worker and likely to take sudden frights. If she got a whiff of a fox, for instance, or suddenly clapped eyes on a bit of red rag fluttering in the hedge, there was no knowing what she might do. Besides Jack and Jill there was the cob, Jamey, who did light farm jobs and always drew the trap, and there were our two ponies that we went to school on, called Ding and Dong. Ding was Sam's and Dong was Beth's and mine. The ponies didn't have to have shoes, but the other three had to be taken regularly to the blacksmith in Martha Tavy, usually by Sam. Since it was four miles each way and there would often be several horses waiting in a queue at the forge, it took a longish time.

''Tis not all that bad though,' Pa said when he'd had a good drink of tea. 'The boy can leave word that we'll be needin' Jim just as soon as we can have 'im. If we're ever going to clear Bull Meadow by nightfall we'll need him and need him bad. Most of that hay'll need turning again 'afore 'tis fit to carry. I'd dearly like to've left it one more day.'

'And what if they're aimin' to carry hay at Bodsworthy today?' asked Granma, who was washing up at the sink. 'If so be they are, I'll warrant they'll be nabbing Jim 'afore you can get 'im.'

Jim was a casual worker living in the village who divided his work between three or four different farms, of which Sunset was one and Bodsworthy was another. He was always in great demand because of his strength. He had helped us with the mowing of Bull Meadow and had ended by mowing over half of it himself.

Pa looked worried. He turned to see the time on the grandfather clock in the corner. It had just chimed half past seven, but no one had noticed because it was such a familiar sound.

'See here, Sam,' Pa said with decision. 'You go straight to Jim's cottage and say I'll pay him double wages for this day so long as rain holds off. That'll settle Bodsworthy. Skinflints they are there. But hurry you up with your breakfast, boy – there's a main of work pilin' up for us today.'

Next thing was, Pa in the middle of his great basin of porridge turned to Ma as if he'd just remembered something.

'Where did 'ee turn them cows after milking – not into Big Mead, I hope?'

'I did not, indeed,' said Ma. 'They're in Little Mead, handy for milkin' tonight. But they'll suffer – an' milk'll go down. 'Tis workin' up to the worst day for flies we've had this summer.'

Usually in midsummer the cows were turned into the Big Mead by day and from there they could go up through two higher fields right out on to the open moor. Once on the moor they could go up and up until they left the flies behind and met the cool breeze of the high tors. But this meant that it might take over an hour to bring them home for milking, so whenever there was hay or corn to bring in, or sheep to be shorn, they had to be put in one of the home fields, where they would be at the mercy of the flies.

I only had one very unimportant part of my mind listening to this kind of farming talk that always went on at our breakfast table. It would be more true to say that I didn't listen to it at all, I only heard it. With most of my mind I was all the time thinking about Sam going in to the village, because I didn't see why I shouldn't go too, since Jack's back could take two children as easily as one.

Ma must have been thinking about this too, because when Pa stopped talking about the hay she said quietly –

'Peter could go along with Sam and take his drawings to Miss Scrimshaw. 'Twill be his last chance before school holidays start.'

I wanted to hug her, but I didn't say a word. I only looked sideways at Beth and saw her face light up.

Pa just went on eating, but since he was thinking I could see there was hope.

'He could have half-an-hour in school and then the two of them could be home by eleven,' Ma went on. "Tis hardly fair to let Sam go and keep Peter home.'

'What about Beth, then?' said Pa, glancing at her. 'That'll not be fair to her either.'

Lots of sisters would have started making a fuss then and clamoured to be allowed to go too. But not Beth. She greatly wanted me to go for my sake. Of course, she did have one reason of her own, too, which was my picture of her that she was madly keen for everyone at school to see. She knew as well as I did that that picture was very special and that it would really make Miss Scrimshaw (even perhaps the schoolmaster too) sit up and take notice.

So Beth said –

'Oh, *please*, Pa, let Peter go. I promise I'll work like anything in the hay if you do – I'll work much harder if you do.'

'Oh you will, eh?' said Pa with a twinkle in his eye. 'And here have I been thinkin' we all of us at Sunset go to it with all our might and main at hay time.'

'Doan't 'ee tease the maid, John,' Ma said. 'Stands to reason she'll work better if she's humoured and so will Peter.'

'We-ell, maybe that's true 'nough,' Pa said, yielding his ground and rather pleased to do it, we could see. Although he added sternly –

'But if I haven't got three children out there in Bull Meadow turning hay with a will by half-past eleven there'll be trouble, I can tell 'ee.'

So breakfast came to a sudden end. I had to nip upstairs to put my school clothes on. Beth rushed off to get my drawings and pack them carefully in my satchel, Sam went out to the stable to fetch Jack. At the last minute I got in a panic about how to explain to the schoolmaster that I could only stay in school half an hour, so Ma had to write out a note for me to take.

When at last we were ready Sam brought Jack to the mounting-block outside the back door and leaped on to his back. It was easy for Sam because he was big for his age and very accustomed to horses. For me it was a long way up, but Sam let me use his foot as a step and so I managed to get myself up behind him without help. Then I got a tight grip round Sam's waist and we were off, at first at a sober walk through the yards because of the hard ground and Jack's missing shoe, but as soon as we were outside in the grass-grown lane Sam urged him into a brisk trot.

3. Miss Scrimshaw

After we had reached the end of Sunset's own grassy lane and had slowed down to a walk on the hard parish road, we heard a horse's hooves coming towards us. Saf pulled Jack off into a gateway to make room as a pony-trap came into sight with one man driving a piebald at a smart trot.

After a good look at the pony, Sam said – ''Tis the doctor.'

The man reined in alongside us and called out –

'Are you boys from Bodsworthy?'

'No, zur, we b'aint,' said Sam, who was always short of words when speaking to the gentry.

So it was up to me. 'We'm Vardens from Sunset,' I said with pride.

The doctor smiled at me and nodded. He was a big man with bushy black side-whiskers and merry eyes.

'Ah, I remember now,' he said. 'And how's that sister of yours that I came to see several times last March?'

'Very well, zur, thank 'ee,' said Sam.

'That's good. You're a healthy lot at Sunset. Except for that little maid of yours I've hardly set foot in your house since the last of you was born.'

Then he asked us our ages. He didn't seem in any hurry now, even though he had been coming up the road at such a speed that his pony was sweating like anything and had a cloud of pestering flies round his head.

'Your father surely hasn't sent you off to school on *that* horse in hay time?' he asked.

'No, zur,' said Sam, 'we be goin' to blacksmith.'

'Ah, I see. Well, I must get on to Bodsworthy, there's a new baby expected there any time now. And I'm afraid there's rain coming – just look at those flies.'

As he gathered up the reins and his pony started to move, he threw back over his shoulder – 'And mind you keep on being healthy at Sunset, for you surely need to, up there on the edge of the beyond.'

When we started off again I said to Sam –

'Did you hear that, Sam – on the edge of the beyond?'

'Aw, that's just gentry-talk,' said Sam scornfully, 'it doan't mean nuthin' to me.'

But it did to me. It linked up with something that had been wandering about in my head ever since the beginning of the school term, when the schoolmaster had made a little speech after the prayers and singing. He had mentioned 'the Great Beyond, where we all go after we die'.

So I tried my thought on Sam.

'If Dartmoor's the beyond, then p'rhaps it's where everyone goes when they die?'

'Naw,' said Sam. 'They goes into ground in churchyard. You'm fair mazed about your old Dartmoor.'

I never much enjoyed conversations with Sam. He never tried to see my point of view, as Beth always did, and I don't think he used his imagination much. But he was strong and brave and knew an awful lot about horses and farming matters.

He knew a lot about Dartmoor, too, and I can see now of course that he was right to call me 'fair mazed' about it.

He had once been with Pa all the way across its centre to the Exeter side of it, so he knew from his own experience that it was really only a limited area of Devon, however wild and frightening it was. But I didn't know that. For me it began just behind our farm and went on and on into endless distances, getting higher and higher and cloudier and cloudier all the time until at last, for all I knew, it might even become part of the sky. For me it really was the Great Beyond.

Since the rest of the way to the village was all on hard ground, Jack had to walk, but it was all downhill, so he walked at a good pace. At Jim's cottage we both dismounted and Sam hooked Jack's bridle rein over the garden gate-post. Then he went in to see Jim (he knew Jim would be at home because he was really more of a small-holder than a labourer, had his own bit of land and two cows and some pigs and never started work for others until he had done his own) while I ran on past the forge and the post office to the school.

At the forge there were two blacksmiths at work and three horses waiting, so I could guess that Sam would have a good half-hour to wait. I was late for school, I knew that, for it must have taken us an hour to reach the village, and school started at eight-thirty. But I didn't mind that, because children like us from the outlying farms were never expected to be very punctual. Those were the days when children still had to take money to school for their education, so parents couldn't be forced to send their children to school at all if they didn't want to. As farmers' children we used to have to take fourpence each to school every Monday, I remember, while the cottagers' and labourers' children had to take twopence.

There were usually about forty children in Martha Tavy school in those days, aged from six or seven to thirteen.

There were two classes, one taken by the schoolmaster and the other by his wife. But on Thursday mornings another special class was taken by Miss Scrimshaw in one of the rooms in the schoolmaster's house.

Our schoolmaster's name was Dodd and he was young and had a big laugh and was very free and easy in his ways. He was popular with everyone and was said to be one of the best village schoolmasters in Devon. I don't remember any of the boys ever giving him any cheek, though the girls sometimes did, which I think was because two of the girls in school were his daughters.

He saw me come in that day and called me up to his desk, so I was able to give him Ma's note at once. He took me straight into Miss Scrimshaw's class, where there were only seven or eight children.

'We've got our little artist,' he said to her, 'but only for half-an-hour, so you must make the most of him. His father needs him for haymaking.'

If I had been especially good at arithmetic, or writing, or Bible-reading and catechism and all that sort of stuff, I feel sure the other children would have disliked me very much. But because I could really *draw* things, I mean things out of my head, and because it was only once a week that I was made a fuss of, they didn't tease me for it and they seemed to think I had a right to be different and to be called an artist. So I could feel, when I came into the room, that the other children were glad I had come, even though I was going to take all Miss Scrimshaw's attention away from them.

Miss Scrimshaw was much older than Mr. Dodd. She had greyish hair and a long white face with big eyes coming out of it – I mean her eyes stuck out in a rather strange way. She was very strict and we were all scared of her because she belonged to the gentry. Her voice was high and distant and her clothes always very expensive. Her skirts rustled silkily and used to sweep across the floor with a great swish.

She made me sit down at the table she used as a desk and spread out on it the drawings I had done since last week. At once she picked out my picture of Beth.

'This is your sister Beth, Peter, is it not?'

'Oh yes, Mam.'

'Has anyone helped you with it?'

'Oh no, Mam.'

'Hm. Well – you've never done anything like *this* before, Peter, have you? Did it take you a long time – an hour, two hours?'

I tried to think back. It was last Sunday in our garden summerhouse. I was at the table with my drawing-pad and crayons and I had made Beth sit quite still on a chair facing away from the sun, which poured in through the open side of the summerhouse. But she hadn't sat there long.

''Bout half-an-hour,' I said.

'Hm – well – if you don't become an artist, Peter, it will be flouting a gift from God.'

'So you think – 'tis a good picture?'

She was looking at me with her bulgy eyes very dark and gleaming.

'What do *you* think?' she suddenly asked, as if I were a grown-up.

'Beth thinks it is,' I said. With all those other children listening and watching, I didn't want to seem proud.

She smiled then, something she very seldom did. 'And we know it is,' she said quietly. Then she propped the picture up on the table and told all the class they could come up and look at it more closely.

I felt really wonderful then, as if it were the best thing that had ever happened to me. No wonder I can remember that day so well. I would have remembered that part of it all my life, even if it hadn't been followed by all that was coming later.

Then Miss Scrimshaw got up, saying that she must take the picture to show to Mr. Dodd and that I was to go with her. But almost as soon as we reached the schoolmaster's desk in the big classroom, that peculiar day proved once again that it was 'a day with a temperature'. Mr. Dodd had risen to his feet when Miss Scrimshaw came in (he always treated her like a very important lady) and we were all three standing looking down at my picture on his desk, when a howling noise started coming in through the windows and doors, which were open because of the heat. Everyone looked up and listened, so for a moment there was no other sound except that noise. Its tone was rather like the wind when it howls round houses on stormy nights, only it was steady and continuous.

One of the bigger boys at the back of the class called out –

'Please zur, 'tis the alarm ziren from the mine.'

At once there was an outburst of excited talking until Mr. Dodd shouted out SILENCE in his loudest voice.

Then he said to the boy who had spoken –

'Your father works in the mine, Walter, doesn't he? If you wish to go home you may do so.'

The mine was in the next village, Mary Tavy, but anything that happened there was almost as important for Martha Tavy.

The siren still sounded and was disturbing the school so much that there didn't seem much hope of settling it down to normal work again. Mr. Dodd and Miss Scrimshaw were talking about it as if they had forgotten me for the moment. Two or three other children asked to be allowed to go home because they had members of their families connected with the mine. There was an undercurrent of excitement flowing all through the school house.

But at last the siren was shut off and Miss Scrimshaw returned to the matter in hand. She always seemed to be in charge of the school on Thursday mornings. She kept Mr. Dodd standing there looking at my picture and then said –

'I'm sure you will understand, Mr. Dodd, what a responsibility you and I now have towards this child. I shall be wanting to have further talk with you on the subject after school.'

Then she turned to me and to my great relief said that I could go home now and leave my picture safely in her hands. I remember she watched me as I walked out. She stood there very stiff and straight, in her long sweeping silky skirts, silently watching me go. That is how I pictured her in my mind's eye for a long time afterwards. She looked so important – she obviously *was* so important – and yet she was watching me, Peter Varden, of Sunset Farm, as if I was important too. Well, that did something for me that must have been both good and bad. It made me happy, of course, but it also put me so much above myself that I was sure to have a bad fall. If I hadn't been put above myself I would probably never have done what I did in the evening of that day. And if it hadn't been for the siren from the Mary Tavy copper mine, Sam and I wouldn't have been late getting home and Jim wouldn't have failed to turn up at Sunset at the right time and Pa wouldn't have been cross, so I wouldn't have had such a strong wish to do what I did in the evening. Everything fitted together on that day to make it *my* unforgettable day. It was the day I grew up, Ma used to say afterwards, because I was never the same afterwards as I was before. Now that I'm as old as I am now, I know that growing up is not an automatic thing at all, not just a matter of adding years together. Some people never grow up at all and some grow up while they are still children.

4. Late for Haymaking

I walked back to the forge through a village very different from usual. It was full of people talking and shouting. Garden gates were open with women talking round them, men were riding up and down on horses and everywhere there was a hum of excitement. Outside the forge I found Sam listening intently to a bunch of old men. When I asked him where our horse was he just jerked his thumb at the forge. I went in and saw Jack in one of the stalls, still with one shoe missing. There was a horse in the other stall with no shoes on at all, but there was no blacksmith working. I felt worried as I rejoined Sam.

Not until the group of men broke up was Sam willing to talk to me. He said that just now a man from Mary Tavy had ridden into the village at the canter, with his horse all in a muck-sweat, and given the news that there had been a rock-fall in one of the mine tunnels and that five men were cut off and would have to be dug out. Strong diggers were needed urgently and both the blacksmiths had already gone. Sam was so excited that he didn't seem to mind at all about not getting Jack done and not getting home at the time we had promised. But I did. I thought it was a shame that the blacksmiths had walked out on their job. I was too young to realise what it meant to have five men walled up in a tunnel underground, with the possibility that all their air would soon be used up or poisoned with gas.

Time went by until even Sam began getting impatient about Jack. At last he plucked up courage to ask one of the old men about it. This man took interest at once, and in a minute the whole group round the door were looking in at the two horses in their stalls and talking about the Vardens' horse still waiting while hay was fit for carrying up at Sunset Farm.

One of the old men went into the forge and started working the bellows with one hand while he raked the fire together with the other, as if he had done it ten thousand times. Then he rolled up his shirt-sleeves and put on a leather apron. Sam and I watched him hopefully.

He asked us which was our horse and then started on Jack. From the way he picked up Jack's foot even I could tell that he had been a blacksmith all his life. When he had pared the hoof he straightened his back painfully and said to us –

'Thee boys should 'a spoke up earlier. Us doan't fancy keepin' Vardens waiting, with hay fit to carry an' all. An' 'tis a fairish way to Sunset.'

He had put just the slightest extra weight on the word 'Vardens', which I noticed at once and felt proud about, but I doubt if Sam did. He didn't usually care about little details like that.

Two or three of the other men had come in now and begun to tease the smith about being too old for his job. It became plain from what they said that he must be the father of the two regular smiths and that he had retired a few years ago after a lifetime's work in that forge. I began to feel much better. Jack was being done properly at any rate and since he had only needed one shoe it surely couldn't take much longer now.

But the old man was like an artist at his work. He kept on applying the hot shoe to Jack's hoof, then taking it away to get it red-hot again for more shaping on the anvil. When it was done to his satisfaction and the nails were all in, he sat down on his anvil and mopped his face with a great red handkerchief. The sweat had been running down his face for some time and even his arms were glistening with it.

Sam went to Jack's head to untie him, but the old man wouldn't let him go yet. He said he would have to examine the other three shoes, because what would our Pa say if Jack got a loose shoe in a week's time?

When we did at last lead Jack out into the village street I had a feeling that it must be awfully late. My tummy, too, was telling me that a long time must have gone by since eight o'clock.

'Let's hurry, Sam,' I said as soon as we were mounted.

'Caw!' said Sam. 'Just you wait. An' if you get scarey I'm not stoppin', mind, so 'twill be no use hollerin'.'

If I had known what I was in for I wouldn't have been fool enough to talk to Sam about hurrying. He wasn't troubled about being late, he was just keen to see if he could get some real speed out of our horse.

Just outside the village he pulled Jack in close to the hedge and broke off a handy switch from an ash tree. Then he told me to hang on very tight and started using the switch lightly on Jack's great rump. Jack was a young horse and had had his fill of standing in a stall that day. As soon as he understood what Sam wanted he got into a canter and really stretched himself, using the grass verge of the road. I had never been so fast before. We both had to hold on for dear life. I had my arms locked round Sam's waist, with my face crushed against his shoulder and could see how fiercely his legs were gripping Jack's sides. I tried to do the same, but mine were not long enough. We passed some people walking and they stopped to stare after us. Further on we saw the doctor's pony-cart coming towards us. When we passed he had halted his pony and was standing up, staring hard, evidently wondering if our horse might be running away with us. But he changed his mind, for he laughed and waved before he disappeared in the distance.

I can still hear the thunder of Jack's great hooves. Although Sam kept him on the grass verge, the ground was baked hard after weeks without rain and the high banks and hedges on both sides boxed in the sound. Sam no doubt was pretending that he was the man sent from Mary Tavy to Martha Tavy with the news about the trapped miners. He would have enjoyed it even more if he had been alone. But I was very frightened. Sometimes when Jack swerved round sharp turns in the road I almost let out a scream.

But we got home safely. That was partly because it was nearly all uphill, and it's much easier to stay on a horse going uphill, especially when you are riding bare-back.

By the time we reached Sunset's own grassy lane Jack had had enough of cantering and Sam was well content to let him do the last three-quarters of a mile at a walk, so that he could cool down. The sun was still blazing and such an awful swarm of flies gathered round the sweating horse as soon as he lost speed that we had to pick sprays of leaves from the hedge and keep waving them round our heads.

Soon we could see our farmstead and the fields rising behind it, so of course we both picked out Bull Meadow to look at first. Sure enough there were people turning hay in it – four altogether, three big and one small. As we got nearer we could see they were Pa and Ma, Granma and Beth. Pa was off on his own, moving fast and making the hay spray out in the air round him, the other three were together, moving slow but steady.

'Where be Jim, then?' For the first time Sam's voice had real worry in it. For Jim had promised he would be at Sunset long before this.

'Maybe havin' his dinner,' I said hopefully. I was thinking about dinner all the time.

Granpa was in the yard waiting for us. Holding Jack's head for us to jump down, he said –

'Make haste inside both of 'ee now, get a bite to eat, and out with 'ee to the hay. Your Pa's frettin' mad.'

'Where's Jim to?' Sam asked.

'Ay, where indeed?' said Granpa severely. 'Just what we've all bin askin' this last hour and more.'

Sam started explaining about the alarm siren, but Granpa cut him short, telling us our dinner must come first. It was all waiting ready for us, he said, little though we deserved it, but we'd be no use in the field with empty bellies. Then he took Jack away to water and feed him.

Granpa had rather subdued us, but not enough to spoil our appetites. Cold lamb and potatoes and cheese, with plenty of milk, we found waiting for us on the kitchen table.

'Tell you what – must 'a happened,' Sam said with his mouth full. ''Twas that there blasted siren – Jim must 'a heard 'un – an's gone off to Mary Tavy.'

I was relieved when I heard this.

''Tis not our fault then, Sam.'

'No, 'taint. Pa'll be fair worried, though.'

As we expected, Granpa came in from the stable before we had finished, partly to hurry us up, but mainly, as we guessed, to hear more about the siren.

'We heard nowt here,' he said with his eyes gleaming with interest. Then he gave us his opinion about mining as he had many times before – how it was unnatural and tempting Providence to go burrowing in the ground like moles and if men did unnatural things they could surely expect trouble. It was a curse on the whole neighbourhood, that mine was, taking good men from the land and wearing them out long before their time. Jim should have had sense enough not to go.

We hardly listened because we'd heard it all before, but at least it gave us a few more minutes at table. He would probably have gone on for some time if we had let him, but as soon as we had stuffed ourselves with food and drink and changed into our older clothes we hurried out to the hay, picking up our prongs and rakes in the cart-shed on our way. We all had different farm tools according to our sizes.

We went straight to Pa, who was still working on his own out in the middle of the field. When he saw us he didn't stop throwing up the hay, though he did slow down a bit. He turned to us a face all streaming with sweat and shouted out – 'Well, boy, what's the story?'

Sam stayed still and began about the siren, but Pa wouldn't have that.

'Get to work, now, both of 'ee. If 'ee can't find breath enough to work as well as talk, after the easy morning ye two've had – well, ye're no proper sons o' mine.'

He was angry and probably he'd been angry a long time, which was why he was making the hay fly in the air so. But as Sam struggled to get our story out, tossing hay at the same time and getting very red and puffed over it, we could see Pa's mood changing and in about ten minutes he was free and easy, interested and full of questions about the trouble in the mine. He never asked about school, though, and I could see I wouldn't be able to tell anything about my picture and Miss Scrimshaw until probably the next day, except of course to Beth.

'One thing certain is,' Pa said when Sam had just about finished, 'we can put no blame on Jim. 'Tis a rare piece o' goodness in a man, to turn his back on a day's work at double wages an' go off to dig out buried men at no wages at all.'

He seemed so much struck by that that he wanted it to be a lesson to me and Sam. Pa was always on the lookout for things that might help to make us good, because he felt guilty about taking us to church so seldom. It was hard luck for him that Granpa had just been saying something so different. But in any case Sam probably felt much the same as I did about Jim, because we had both seen how Martha Tavy village street had buzzed with new life after the siren and how all the people seemed to be waking up and enjoying themselves. We felt that what had taken Jim off to the mine might not have been all goodness; about half of it might have been just excitement and wanting to play a part in important things.

Looking back on that day from this end of my life, I can pick out easily now where Jim really showed his goodness. He showed it in turning up at Sunset after tea-time, on a pony he had borrowed, after hours of heavy pick-and-shovel work down in the mine. But that comes a bit later in my story.

The sun stayed out till mid-afternoon and that hayfield was like an oven. There wasn't the faintest breeze and the flies buzzing round our heads were almost more than we could bear. If we got puffed and worked with our mouths open, flies would go in every minute or so and we would have to spit hard to get them out – if we had been lucky enough to prevent them going down our throats. There was the sound of our spitting all round the field and also of Pa swearing, for flies in the mouth was the one thing that really made him swear.

When the sun went in and Pa stopped to have a good look at the sky, we were glad to stop, too, and throw ourselves down on the ground. A strange-looking wall of clouds had been very slowly rising all over the southern part of the sky and had at last swallowed the sun.

'He's gone,' Pa said, mopping his brow and neck. 'An' maybe we'll not see 'un again for many a long day. He's done well by us and no mistake. This here's the sweetest field o' hay we're likely to see in half a lifetime. And now we'll carry 'un by nightfall – or else –'

He didn't finish his sentence, but swept his eye round the field, then up to the high moors and tors in the distance, then back to Ma and Granma and Beth, who had stopped, too, and were sitting down resting near the hedge.

'You two boys go for the horses,' he said then, quick and snappy. 'Put Jill in the new cart and Jack in the old and be back here *sharp*. And ropes, mind – see there's a rope for each cart. Off you go now – I'm starting to rake up.'

Sam and I ran. Our arms were tired and aching pretty badly, at least mine were, but our legs were fine and we needed to stretch them. I couldn't keep pace with Sam, of course. By the time I was through the second gate he was half way across the third field and when I reached the stable he already had the collar and hames on Jill. Granpa had heard us and came to help me harness up Jack, for some of it I couldn't manage. When both horses were in the shafts Granpa fetched two baskets already packed with food and two jugs of cider from the house, dumped them in Jack's cart and then climbed in himself. He sat himself down on the floor, which meant that he was leaving the driving to me. I was pretty quick scrambling up on to the front of the cart and picking up the reins, for I was hoping to be first back in the hayfield. Sam had gone into the house for a drink, but when he heard my cart's iron-rimmed wheels rumbling through the yard he came out running. I kept ahead of him through the first field, but in the second he made Jill trot and overtook me easily.

We couldn't have been away more than a quarter of an hour, but there was a row of hay raked up already, reaching right across the field from the gate to the farther headland. They were all raking, Pa working like a demon and just starting on a second row. It made me feel a bit tired to see them and I wondered especially how tired Beth might be. I hadn't had a chance to talk to her yet, though I wanted to badly.

When they saw the carts they all stopped raking and began coming towards us. Granpa had got out and was kicking the hay about, picking up handfuls here and there to test it.

''Tis *barely* fit an' no more,' he said to Pa who reached us first.

'Well, 'tis coming in, whether or no,' said Pa. 'And coming in fast. See that sky?'

'I reckon 'twill not rain till sundown,' Granpa said, eyeing that wall of black clouds in the south. 'That's movin', but movin' good an' slow. Us'll have wind first – till that come we'm safe.'

I knew Pa wouldn't rest for a moment now until the first load was up. There wasn't much hope of that lovely family picnic tea that we usually had together in the hayfields when the weather was settled.

'Be you makin' first load, Fayther?' Pa called. 'Up you get now, for I'm startin' pitchin'.'

He had shoved his prong into the row of hay and pushed it along the ground until he had a little mountain close to one of the carts. Then he heaved it up and brought it down with a great clomping swoosh, smiling as he did so. This was the moment he had been dying for the whole day, when the first bit of this lovely hay was made safe against all the tricks of our moody Dartmoor climate.

Granpa said nothing, but grabbed a special short prong and climbed in amongst the hay, at once starting to tramp it down under his feet.

5. Carrying Hay at Sunset

All this had happened while Ma and Beth and Granma were still coming towards us. When they reached us their first thoughts were on the baskets that Sam and I were taking out of the other cart. But my first thoughts were for Beth.

Sam went off to help pitch, but the rest of us lay down round the baskets. I sat next to Beth, of course, but still I couldn't talk to her about the picture and Miss Scrimshaw because I had to tell our story of the morning, all about the siren and the long wait for Jack's shoe and all the rest of it. I was a bit tired by this time and couldn't tell it as well as Sam, so they had to get most of it out of me by questions. We were all eating and drinking fast, too, knowing that Pa might start hollering at us to get working again at any moment.

It only seemed like five minutes before that first loaded cart was coming towards us, though it must have been quite a bit longer than that really. It was Jill's cart and Pa was leading her. When she had a heavy load behind her she was always mettlesome and in need of a firm hand on the bridle. In those days we used two-wheel tip-carts for our hay carrying, so that when the cart reached the place where it was to be unloaded all you needed to do was to take off the rope, unfasten the tail-board which held the back lade and then start the cart tipping until the whole mass of hay slid on to the ground. But this was the first load, so it did not slide off on to the ground but on to the stack-bottom of faggots and straw which had been got ready for it in the field near the gate. We always stacked our hay in the fields instead of taking it down at once into the yards. It made more work in winter, but it meant that we could carry our hay quicker.

Before tipping, Pa turned Jill round and backed her until the cart-wheels just touched the edge of the faggots.

It was usually Ma's job to build the stack. (It was more often called a mow in those days). So as soon as that first cart had been tipped she got up rather stiffly to start spreading out the great mound of hay all over the stack bottom. Building the stack was less hard work than any of the other jobs. There wasn't any heavy lifting involved in it and if you could have someone else up on the stack with you, to keep pushing the hay towards you as it came off the prong of the pitcher, then building could be great fun, though at the same time a skilled operation with great responsibilities. A badly built stack could slip sideways and not only cause a tremendous lot of extra work but also let the rain in and ruin a lot of hay.

Granma went to help Ma, so at last I had a chance to talk to Beth. We got up too, so as to look as if we were going to start work, but Jack and the other cart being so conveniently close beside us, we both got the same idea at the same moment – we slipped out of sight between them and the hedge.

'What about my picture, Peter?'

''T was – oh, 't was – wondrous,' I said, close to her ear. 'She picked it out straight off and kep on looking at it – sort of strange-like. A bit flummoxed by it, she was –'

'Did she know 'twas me?'

''*Course* she did – everyone did. An' she said I've *got* to be an artist now, else God'll be fair put out.'

'Oh my, Peter, did she say that?'

'She did, truly she did. An' then she made all the class come up and see it close.'

'Was Maisie there? Did *she* see it?'

I had to think for a moment. The truth was I had hardly noticed who had been in Miss Scrimshaw's class that day, because I hadn't sat down with them.

'I think so,' I said, guessing.

Then I told how Miss Scrimshaw had taken it to Mr. Dodd. But when Beth wanted to know what he in his turn had had to say about it, I found I couldn't answer. He seemed to have said nothing, but only nodded at everything Miss Scrimshaw had said.

'And did *he* show it to his class too?' Beth asked.

'The siren came then. But after it stopped – and after I'd gone – then he must 'a done, o' course.'

'How d'you know, if you'd gone?'

'Stands to reason he would – or *she* would, more like. 'Tis such a good picture, Beth, she said so. 'Tis much, much, much better'n we thought!'

'Oh, if *only* I'd been there! An' how I do wish this day was over. Then p'raps we can go to school tomorrow and I can talk to Maisie about it.'

I tried to think about her instead of me.

'Are you terrible tired, Beth?'

Her eyes didn't look it, because they were lit up with what I'd been telling her, but her face did. It was white and blotchy and her chestnut hair was bedraggled and soaked with sweat in places. She was usually so beautiful, but now only her eyes were. No one would know she was the girl in our picture. (I always tried to think of it as our picture when I was with her).

'I've sort of gone past it,' she said. 'My arms ached cruel bad this morning, but now I don't feel 'em much – they sort of go on without me. Oh, look, Peter, there's Granma comin'.'

'God bless my soul, hidin' away there when there's work clamourin' to do! That's not Varden ways –'

Granma's voice had had its cutting edge freshly sharpened, no doubt by the flies and the heat and the tiredness. She was very likely the most tired of all. But since she never had any pity on herself, we couldn't really expect her to have much pity on us.

'Look at your Pa – don't 'ee want to please a man that can master his work in such a fashion as that?' she said more kindly when we came out into the open. But we didn't need nor really want to look at him, because we knew so well what he was like when carrying hay. He would do the work of two men and even joke and laugh and seem to be enjoying himself, and then as soon as he finished for the day he would be like a man struck dumb and would drop into a chair and nod off to sleep instead of eating his supper.

He had a second load nearly finished and we knew we were needed for raking up another row. We joined Granma on the job and then Ma, as soon as she had spread out all the first load over the stack bottom, came to work alongside us until she should be wanted again for building. Now that the sun had gone it was less terribly hot, but the flies tormented us worse than ever.

As Beth had said, when you are working in a hay field you sooner or later get past the aching stage and become a sort of numb clockwork thing that almost forgets how to stop. Then when you do stop all your aches and pains come to life again and quite likely make you a bit angry about everything, about having to work so hard and be so pestered by heat and flies – especially when you are very young and know you won't have any time left to play before bedtime.

When we did have our next stop Beth and I were tired enough to be a little bit angry and rebellious. We stopped because Pa called to us from the stack, where he had just finished pitching the fourth or fifth load. He wanted Jack and the other cart to be brought into action, which meant re-arranging our work. One of us would have to make the load on Jack's cart while Sam pitched to it. So it was an opportunity for us all to have a drink and for Pa and Granpa to inspect the stack and let Ma know if she was building it rightly. By now it was three feet high, smelling like a cow's idea of heaven and inviting you to throw yourself down on it and go straight off to sleep.

Beth and I climbed on to it and lay down beside Ma, who smiled at us sympathetically. I think she was awfully tired herself.

When Pa started fretting to have us all working again, Ma stood up and said she must have someone to help on the stack. She didn't ask, she simply said it in the tone to make Pa know that it would be no use arguing about it. Beth and I flashed a hopeful glance at each other. Helping on the stack was much the nicest of all haymaking jobs.

'Take Peter then,' Pa called. 'Beth can make a load an' he can't!'

I felt this was a bit unfair to Beth, but we'd learned by now that fairness didn't count in the hay field. The only thing that counted was the quickest way to get the work done.

Beth made a face as she slid down off the stack. 'No more rakin', that's something,' she said, but she gave me an envious look. We were feeling the lack of Jim now, very badly. If he were there to do the second cart's load and pitch it to the stack, everything would go at twice the speed. He was a better pitcher even than Pa and that was saying a lot. Granma was out in the field again, raking steadily as if she could go on for hours yet. Nearly half the field was in rows now.

Ma and I had a little time still to rest, since there was no load waiting at the stack. We stayed lying there in that sweet-smelling feather bed. She was nearly asleep, I think, but I didn't feel a bit sleepy. I wanted her to ask about school and Miss Scrimshaw. I was aching a lot and still a bit angry about everyone thinking so much about hay and so little about what had happened to me that morning. So I started to talk, not realizing that it was unkind of me.

'Ma, does it matter so *terribly* much, gettin' all this hay in before dark comes?'

She seemed surprised and sat up to look down at me.

'Yes, Peter, it *does* matter terribly. If it rains now it'll go right on raining for weeks, off and on, 'tis bound to after all the lovely weather we've had. This hay'll go black and be only fit for bedding or p'raps even for burning. Pa will blame hisself cruel for not getting up earlier in the morning and p'raps even for letting you go off to school. An' we'll not have enough to get the cows through the winter. The poor beasts'll come into the shippen some raw February day and find nowt but straw in their mangers and – they'll look round at us with their big eyes all sad and accusin' – oh, I can't abide that, Peter. I can't abide it an' I'll do anything to save us from it happening. Pa's right to drive us on so. Maybe it does hurt a bit now, but 'tis only to save us from worse hurting in the winter-time.'

I hadn't expected she would get so worked up. It was a

shock to me. Her words sank in and started things changing round inside me. Being an artist, handling pencils and crayons and lovely sheets of white paper, and having people admiring pictures I had drawn – all that began to get smaller and smaller and fade away into the distance. What moved into its place and got bigger and bigger was being a farmer's son and handling hay and horses and cows. It was a little like waking up from a dream. Sunset Farm was the real world and Miss Scrimshaw and my picture were the dream world.

Ma went on talking. Perhaps it had been a shock to her to find me not caring enough about the farm or not understanding enough. Ma was always the one who explained things and you had to listen to her if you wanted to learn. With Pa you learned by just watching him. This was what Sam found easiest. He could learn best from Pa while I could from Ma.

She went on to say that losing this hay would be a double blow to Pa. He had a name in the parish as a good farmer and if talk started going round about the Vardens having lost their best hay, and in a fine summer too, he would be cut to the quick. So would they all be. They hadn't had any hay 'gone to muck' at Sunset for two or three years, not in fact since we children had become old enough to work in the fields. Nor had they, for two or three years, run as big a risk as they had been running all day with this field. Such a thick heavy crop it was, too. If only they had cut it two days earlier none of this trouble would have happened. But then how could anyone know when the weather was going to break? There were some things you simply had to trust to luck for and hay was one.

'Oh Ma, do you think we *will* carry all the field in time?' I asked, being a serious farmer now and likely to remain one until the artist came slinking back again through a side door.

'It'll be a miracle if we do, Peter. The sky's lookin' real bad now. But if we get a drop or two of rain first, to warn us, Pa'll stop carryin' and start putting the rest in pokes and that'll partly save it.'

Pokes are little hay cocks that you pile up in the field and which can take a few days of rain without a lot of damage.

An idea came to me then.

'There's one thing *I* could do, Ma. I could go for the cows and start milking on my own.'

She looked at me close, wondering if I really meant it. I had never done it alone and was frightened of it as soon as I'd suggested it. Until now I had always refused to go without Beth.

'That would be a help, sure 'nuff,' she said. 'To have those cows all inside and being milked when we leave work here – because there'll be no stoppin' for us till dark, that's certain, without rain to force it. We'll see what Pa says to it.'

He was just pulling in to the stack with another load, but before we could ask him about the cows our attention was drawn towards the gate where there was a sound of trotting hooves. Jim came riding into the field with a grin on his face, hopped off his pony and hitched him to the hedge, then strode up to the stack.

He put his hands on his hips and cocked his head at Pa.

'Got any work for I, maister?'

He looked very well pleased with life, as if just returned from a holiday outing. He was a tall man with a round freckled face and close-cropped ginger hair. His arrival was like the sun coming out again.

Pa tipped the load, then handed his long hay prong to Jim.

'Never was better pleased to see a man in all my born

days,' Pa said with a wide smile. Then he went to the jugs of cider and poured some drinks.

Jim dug his prong into the edge of the tipped load, pressed it far in with his foot, then brought the handle right down until its top met the ground, with a huge mass of hay rising on the other end. One great heave brought the prong upright, with the hay in the air above his bent back, and another heave sent it flying on to the stack. That done, to prove that he was ready for hard work, he was also ready for a drink and a snatch of talk.

Granpa, standing beside him, said –

'So that there old mine couldn't keep 'ee long from the hay, seemin'ly?'

'Any field I mows I reckons to carry too,' said Jim grandly. 'Besides,' he added, "tis workin' up for streams o' rain. Happen this be one time I wouldn't be here else, for I'm fair tired, I can tell 'ee.'

'They'm rescued then, they miners?' Pa said, handing him a mug of cider.

'Naw, they b'aint yet,' said Jim, 'but they'm safe.'

He told them how, after hours of hard digging, the trapped men had been heard tapping about noon and how it had then been possible for a steel tube to be drilled through to them, through which they could speak and get plenty of air. Except for one man who had had a foot crushed under a boulder, they were all well and had food and drink enough to keep them going. The rest of the digging would have to go slow for fear of more rockfalls, but it was expected they would be got out tomorrow.

Then he went straight back to his pitching and everyone went to work so quick that my idea of fetching the cows was not mentioned. Pa put Jill into a trot and was away across the field for another load before I knew what was happening. The hay was coming on to the stack so fast from Jim's pitching that poor Ma would have been nearly buried if I hadn't struggled all I could to help her. When Jim finished that load and went off into the field we had a few minutes to get our breath, so we watched to see what Pa would want Beth to do. Jim took over from Sam as pitcher for Jack's cart and Sam took over from Beth as load maker. Would Beth come on to the stack to help Ma and so let me go for the cows? I knew it must be well past their usual time for being brought in.

Ma and I watched Beth jump down from her half-finished load and go off to the hedge to get her rake. Then she joined Granma on the distant part of the field that had not yet been raked into rows.

I was sad, but Ma said –

'That job's nearly done and she'll surely come then.'

When Pa came in with another load he and Ma had a little discussion about how things were going and how much daylight there was left. The upshot of that was that when he had pitched that load up and got back on to his cart he shouted out very loud –

'Soon as raking's done, Beth go and help Ma, and Peter go for cows – an Mother can go on home.'

How proud I was then! It was the first time I had ever been given that order and to have it shouted like that to be heard all over the field made me feel so grown up, such a valuable member of a team that was doing important and urgent work.

I suppose it was half-an-hour later, with the light noticeably failing, when we saw Beth and Granma walking towards us with their rakes over their shoulders. I started down the ladder at once (the stack was high enough now to need one) asking Ma as I went if I could have a drink of cider.

'You can this once,' she called, so I poured myself a good mugful.

As I ran off, Ma shouted after me –

'Take Toby with you, but don't let him drive those cows.'

Toby was our best sheepdog, but he was no good with cows. Sheepdogs seldom are, unless they're old, because they like to get them running like sheep and cows hate that. But Ma knew I was rather scared about going alone and that Toby would be company for me.

6. Going for the Cows

To get to Little Mead it was easiest to go down to the farmyard and then up again through the orchard. The apple trees in our orchard were mostly very old and had been allowed to grow up much taller than they ought to be. From Bullmeadow it was therefore not possible to see across to Little Mead, nor to any of the other fields beyond the orchard except the higher ones up towards the moor, because the apple trees were in the way and made a tall screen of green leaves. So all through the day, although we had taken it for granted that the cows were in the Little Mead, none of us had actually had a glimpse of them.

I ran all the way downhill to the farmyard. The daylight was getting dim and I was very set on my idea of having at least some of the cows milked before darkness brought the haymakers in from their work.

Toby was easy to find, asleep in his special corner in the stable. He had such a thick coat that he suffered in hot weather and used to lie about dozing and lazing on roastingly hot days. But he came to life very quick when he saw that I was inviting him to come with me up through the orchard. No doubt he thought I wanted him for sheep.

On my way through the yard I also picked up my special stick that I always used when Beth and I fetched the cows.

Pa used to say no one should go after bullocks (bullocks was the word we used for any sort of horned stock except sheep) without a good stick and especially children should not, because young bullocks often get frisky and start playing games with you. They never mean any harm, but it's no fun being prodded by a horn even in play.

I expect it was partly that long drink of cider that made me feel so good as I tramped up through the orchard, with my stout stick pushing me on and with Toby trotting at my heels. I was a double boy just then. The artist had come back inside me, but had not pushed the farmer's son out of the way. Instead he was saying to the farmer's son – 'I'm glad you'm a fine young Varden that thinks nothin' o' going out at the end of a day to fetch in Sunset's cows,' while the farmer's son was saying to the artist – 'I'm glad you'm there, 'cause there be lots of things about Vardens and Sunset farm that need special eyes to look at 'em an' see what they're really like.'

In the top corner of the orchard hedge, not far from the gate into Little Mead, there were some holly trees which had become smothered in ivy. The thick mass of dark green holly and ivy leaves all tangled up together made a place where it was always twilight even in sunshine. This was the day-time home of a special friend of mine and Beth's and we never went through the orchard without going to see him and passing the time of day with him. We had come to believe that it would be very unlucky to pass through without visiting him. This evening I very nearly did because of having so much on my mind, but I remembered just in time. Looking up into the darkest part of the holly trees I could just make out, after staring hard, two round eyes that stared into mine.

'Hullo, Mr. Owl,' I said. 'I'm going to get the cows

in, so I mustn't stay. I hope you have good hunting to-night.'

Beth and I had discovered him last year, quite by chance, and had visited him many times. He was nearly always there. If we went too close or touched the lower branches of the trees he used to blink his eyes and sometimes even disappear without a sound and come into sight again on the wing some distance away on the other side of the hedge. We always called him *Mr.* Owl. It is a strange thing that owls always seem to get treated with respect. As soon as darkness came he would probably be off to Bullmeadow, where all the hay carting would have left the field-mice without any protective covering.

When I reached the gate into Little Mead I unlatched it and let it swing open before I realised there was anything wrong. Then I entered the field and turned to look at the only part of it that had not been visible from the gate. There were no cows there.

'Oh,' I said, out loud. 'What shall we do now, Toby?'

I used to talk a lot to myself, or to animals, when I was alone out-of-doors.

Toby stood beside me, still panting with the heat, wagging his tail, looking round the field and then back to my face as if to say – I'm at your service, but where are the sheep? An empty field is no good to *me*.'

I had to use my brains. This was what Pa always told us to do when anything went wrong on the farm. 'Don't do the first thing that comes to mind,' he would say. 'Happen t'will be the second or third thing that serves 'ee best.'

The first thing I thought of was to run back to Bullmeadow. But that wouldn't do, because they would ask me at once if I had looked into the next field. So I walked across to the farther headland and climbed the high bank with the hedge on top of it which surrounded the field. Toby scrambled up beside me and together we surveyed the whole of the next field. It was empty, so again I thought of running back to the hay field. But then, my reason told me, the cows must have got out of Little Mead either through a gate or through the hedge. One gate I had found latched, so now I must go to the other one between Little Mead and the field adjoining. I found it closed and latched.

'Then there's a gap in the hedge,' I said aloud to myself, although Toby thought I said it to him. The gap was easy to find. There was a place where several large stones had slipped down out of the bank. Here the cows had evidently climbed up and pushed through the hedge above, scattering a lot of loose dry earth in the process. Probably the flies had maddened them so that they had kept pushing at a weak place until something had given way. I went through the gap with Toby and out into the adjoining field. Then suddenly I realised where I was and just how serious the trouble might be.

The field I was in now was the Mid Mead. It was next door to Big Mead, with the gate open between the two. So it was one of the fields the cows went through to get out on to the open moor, when they were put in Big Mead. Certainly then they had gone out to the moor today and probably they had gone unusually far over the moor since the flies had been so frightfully bad. They *might* of course be on their way home now, as it was so long after milking time – but on the other hand they might not. So again I had to use my brains.

First, I thought, I must run back as fast as possible and get Dong, because it would take so long to walk all the way out to the moor and anyway we always used the ponies for that job. It was so much more fun and ponies were better than human legs for rounding up the cows if they were scattered over the moor. Then my second thought came. If I went back for Dong I would have to go to the stable to fetch a bridle and I would almost certainly be seen by Granma. Or if she did not see me fetching the bridle she would certainly hear Dong coming through the yards, which was the way I would have to ride him to get to Big Mead. She would yell out to know what I was up to and when she found out she would never let me ride out to the moor alone at this time of day. She would tell me to fetch Sam and let *him* go. It would be the end of my first chance to get the cows in alone, my first chance to do something really valuable towards helping the family to carry all that hay before dark.

So my third thought was, I would just go on up on foot until I found the cows, After all, it was still daylight, even though it did seem to be getting dark much earlier than usual, and I had Toby with me. In a case like this it would be the right thing to let a sheepdog round up the cows. Even if he did start them running too fast and put them in a bad temper, that would be better than having darkness come down before they could all be found.

I ought to have had a fourth thought, but how can any boy be expected to think of everything? Besides, for this fourth thought you really needed more experience of cows' habits than I could have had at my age.

The fourth one was this. Supposing the cows had returned from the moor on their own, which was very probable because it was already so long after their usual time for milking? Then would they have gone back through the gap in the hedge into Little Mead or would they have carried on as they usually did, down to the end of Big Mead where the gate was through which they were usually fetched? Of course they would do the second thing and that meant there was a good possibility they were all at this moment waiting quietly round the Big Mead gate, where I couldn't see them. I ought to have scrambled up the bank and taken a quick look through the hedge into Big Mead.

But I never thought of it. I walked at a good pace up through the two last and highest fields on the farm, keeping Toby close beside me. Near the last gateway we entered a dwarf forest of bracken which would be mown after harvest and carted down to the yards for winter bedding. It reached up to my shoulders and would have been difficult to walk through if there had been no trampled path made by the cows. There was probably a smell of rabbits, for I could not keep Toby at my heels on the path. He went off sniffing with his head down into the forest. I heard him give a sudden excited yelp and start running like mad, though all I could see were the bracken tops waving this way and that. Then I heard a rabbit screaming.

I stopped and called to Toby, but he didn't come. Evidently he had caught a rabbit, which did not please me at all. It was an extra worry just at the moment when I had so many other worries to cope with. While waiting for him and calling to him I looked down over the whole farm, being high above the screen of orchard trees now. Because of the high banks and hedges round the fields it was only possible to see the centres of them. In Bullmeadow I could see one of the horses and carts moving out in the middle, so I knew they must be still at work there. I could see the middle of Big Mead but not the bottom corner where I ought to have looked to see if the cows could be waiting. I could see thick blue smoke rising from one of the farmhouse chimneys (which meant that Granma was coaxing the fire back to life in the kitchen in order to cook an evening meal) and

I could see how strangely dark and heavy the clouds were, all over the low country towards Tavistock. Instead of a sunset happening down there, there seemed to be something rising, something evil and threatening. There was a wind coming from there too, a gusty intermittent wind which was teasing the clusters of young berries in some rowan trees growing on the field boundary.

It was nice to be able to look down and see them all in Bullmeadow, even though they were far away, far beyond calling distance. The light was failing so much now that I could not tell how much of the field still remained to be cleared, but I *could* see that the haystack was tall enough to show up above the hedgerow bushes.

Since Toby would not come to me I would have to go to him. Moving bracken-tops showed me where he was, but it was hard work pushing my way through the forest.

When I reached him he was lying down with the rabbit between his jaws. He looked up at me and wagged his tail, very pleased with himself. But when I reached out to pick up the rabbit he growled so fiercely that I drew my hand away very quickly. It was a young rabbit, about half-grown, big enough to make a real feast for any sheepdog. Its eyes were bursting out of their sockets as if they were screaming inside. I felt such a pang of pity for the rabbit that I would have got it away from Toby and let it go, if I could, which would have been very silly, for it was already more than half dead and that would only have made it die more slowly.

'I'm very sorry, bunny,' I said out loud. 'But I can't help you at all.'

It was hard luck for me, having to stand there looking down at that poor little rabbit. It would have been wiser to go on without Toby at once, as soon as that yelp told me what he had found, because there never was any possibility that I could take the rabbit away from him. Sheepdogs are tame only up to a certain point and there are some things that children cannot do to them. Pa would have been able to, I expect, but only by speaking very sternly. I did make one more attempt, but his growl was angrier than the first time. But at least it made him close his jaws so tight that I knew the rabbit must die. I could hear its ribs breaking up in his teeth.

I was trying hard to use my brains again, that's why I stayed there watching Toby's rabbit. Why had I at once wanted to take it from him, even before it looked at me with those screaming eyes? Because if Toby kept it he would stay there to eat it and afterwards he would want to go to sleep and would be in no mood for going out on the moor with me. So his catching that rabbit meant that I would have to leave him behind. I didn't want to, of course. I hated the idea so much that I lingered there glued to the spot, looking down in horrified fascination at what Toby was doing and still racking my brains for some way of getting over this difficulty. The truth was that I was afraid to go on alone, badly afraid, and it was partly what had happened to the rabbit that was making me afraid.

Usually I lived in such a kind safe world. My family and the farm and all the animals on it were kind and safe and ordinary. Even when something extraordinary happened, like those men getting trapped in the mine, still they were soon going to be rescued – and just think what a great fuss and effort had been made over them, as soon as the alarm had sounded.

And now suddenly I was having a glimpse of a world that was not kind or safe or ordinary at all, a world in which you could quite easily find yourself between the jaws of a beast far bigger than you and have your bones and your heart crunched up by great teeth.

These were the thoughts that flashed through my mind as I stood there looking down at Toby starting his meal. He of course was blissfully happy. But although I usually liked him so much, I could not share any of his happiness now. I was on the side of the rabbit.

But nobody else seemed to be, not even God. That rabbit had been absolutely alone and unprotected, and yet the vicar in his sermon in Martha Tavy church on Easter Sunday had talked about God always being there to take care of every living thing on earth, even the sparrows – and now here I was looking down at this poor creature who had screamed for help and hadn't been given any. Could it really be true, what the vicar had said?

'Poor bunny,' I said out loud. It was easier to speak to him now that he was very certainly dead. 'God was not taking care of *you* when Toby got you, that's certain sure. An' if your ma was, she wasn't doing it very well. P'raps you went too far from home?'

You can see why I was so afraid and why I stood there so long thinking. Supposing I was going too far from home, too? Wouldn't it be the sensible thing to go back now, to forget about Toby and the rabbit and the cows and the hay and just turn round and run like the wind all the way downhill through the fields the orchard and the yards and up again to Bullmeadow and tell Ma and Beth on the stack what had happened and let them sort it out the best way they could?

And then I started thinking of how Sam would immediately rush off for Ding and ride him like mad up through these fields which I had just come through and then out on to the moor and have those cows rounded up in no time and bring them down at the run, shouting at them and enjoying himself like anything. And I would feel defeated. What was more, it would be a double defeat, one for the farmer's son and one for the artist.

No, it would be too unpleasant, I really could not face that. Not yet, at any rate, not until I had gone a bit farther and reached the last gateway, the one where the farm ended and the open moor began.

So that was how I decided at last, at the end of those long minutes watching Toby with his rabbit. I had a clear choice between two very unpleasant things, one to go on at least as far as the last gateway, called the moorgate, and the other to go back and admit defeat. And I decided that the second would be worse than the first. This is very often the reason why people do things that are called brave – because they cannot bear the pain of admitting defeat.

As I pushed my way back through the bracken forest to the cows' path I called to Toby several times, but as I expected, it was in vain. I was looking ahead hopefully now to the moor-gate, expecting at any moment to see one of the cows coming through it. I was reminding myself too of the many times recently that Beth and I had ridden up here on the ponies. I told myself that nothing would be any different from usual just because I was alone, that in fact there was not anything to be afraid of at all. I remembered with satisfaction that, in spite of my hurry, I had gone out of my way to stop and pass the time of day with Mr. Owl as I went up through the orchard. So no bad luck was to be expected from that direction.

At last I reached the moor-gate, the place where Sunset farm ended. Until this point, the encircling high boundary wall of earth and stone, with its stunted ash and thorn trees growing on top of it, had prevented me from seeing anything of the slopes of Dartmoor beyond. Now I went through the open gateway and stopped dead in surprise.

There was nothing there! The moors really had become the Great Beyond. There was nothing but grey fog swirling and writhing in the wind, no tors, no skyline, no cows, nothing. In the distance there was a moaning sound, which must be the wind among the invisible rocks of the nearest tor.

I stared and stared – and listened and listened. Where *could* those cows be? Did I dare to call them? They might be quite close, perhaps lying down in a bunch just inside the grey curtain of fog. But could I raise my voice and call them in such a great silence and emptiness as I could feel all round me? Supposing some other sort of creatures, not cows at all, came out of that misty Beyond in answer to my call? Creatures like – well, wolves, for instance – or those phantom hounds that Dartmoor legends say can be heard howling in full cry over the moor on stormy nights.

How I longed for Toby at that moment! I would only need to say the right word and wave my arm at the fog and he would be away like an arrow from the bow. If there were any sheep or bullocks to be found anywhere in the neighbourhood of the moor-gate he would round them up, fog or no fog, and have them running through that gateway towards the farm in less than a quarter of an hour.

But what could *I* do? It seemed that I was in for another two or three minutes of agonized thinking, while all the time the daylight was steadily failing and I was getting more and more lonely. And then I heard a cow moo-ing not far away in the fog.

7. In the Jaws of the Fog

I was pleased to hear that cow. It was such a familiar reassuring sound that at once it gave me courage enough to call out as loud as I could, trying to make my call sound as much as possible like the usual calls that Beth and I, and sometimes Ma, used for the cows. My voice did not sound quite right, of course. It quavered a bit at first, but I was able to improve it and the cow helped me by answering, or seeming to. I could not tell which cow it was, but that did not worry me because it seemed likely enough that the cows' voices as well as mine might sound strange in this thick fog.

The cow did not seem to be coming any closer, so I went towards her, entering the fringe of the fog. She moo-ed again and I went on towards her, wanting very badly to get near enough to see her so that I could have something nice and safe and familiar to use my eyes on, instead of that horrible grey fog.

To leave the safety of the moor-gate and go off into that fog was almost as silly as to walk with open eyes into one of Dartmoor's quaking bogs, which are always quite easy to recognise by their bright green colour. It was not as if fogs were something unknown to me. I had been in them once or twice before, though of course never alone nor late in the evening. I had been told often enough that they were dangerous, far more dangerous than bogs. I am still surprised even now, when I look back down the years and see that solitary boy staring and listening at the moor-gate, with darkness gathering and a sinister wind moaning over the invisible tors. I still have to ask myself, how *could* he have been so foolish as to leave the moor-gate, to let it go out of his sight even for a single moment?

For a long time afterwards I used to pretend that it was the cow's fault, but I never really believed it myself and nor of course did anyone else. It was true she kept moo-ing at intervals as if she were answering me, but in fact, as I was very soon to discover, she was minding her own business in proper cow fashion. It is also true that if she had not been there at all I would not have gone into the fog. But the deeper truth is that I was so frightened and so lonely that I wanted that cow for her comforting familiar presence. That's part of the explanation. Another part of it is that, since I took it for granted that the moo-ing cow was one of ours, I was sure that the whole Sunset herd must be just there, close beside me though hidden by the fog and I had a great desire therefore to get among them quickly and start them moving for home.

Then there is yet another part of the explanation, and a very simple one it is too, though no one seemed to notice it then. This is, that we are all of us likely to do unexpectedly foolish things when we are seriously overtired. My day had started at a quarter to five and that was by now a good sixteen hours ago. And what a day it had been! So you see I had plenty of excuses for doing that utterly foolish thing.

Well, I walked away from the moor-gate into the fog. It was probably about a quarter of an hour after sunset on a dark evening, so I had at the very most one hour left before total darkness closed in. Today, in similar circumstances, most boys would have a compass in their pockets, and know how to use it. But I did not even know that such things existed.

I was walking over the usual sort of Dartmoor ground – coarse grass, heather, bracken, gorse, with outcrops of rock here and there. I had a clear enough view of what lay before my feet and for about seven or eight paces beyond. Everything else was swallowed up in fog.

I could hear the cow's movements before I actually saw her. She was so close that her next moo nearly made me jump into the air. Then she was suddenly there before my eyes, standing right in my way and looking at me with keen interest. She was black all over, very big and fat, obviously completely harmless and gentle in spite of her big horns. I had never seen her before.

Perhaps she also was disappointed, for after a good look and a good smell at me she just turned right round and went off the way she had come, lifting her nose for another moo into the fog. I was so amazed and horrified that I just stood there gaping.

She must be one of the beef cows belonging to a big farmer down at Martha Tavy. I had forgotten all about them. They used to be turned out on to the moor in May, with their calves running beside them, to spend the whole summer up there roaming about where they liked. This one must have lost her calf in the fog.

As I stood there trying to collect my wits I heard an unmistakable calf's voice answering her. Just to make sure, I went forward a little in the direction she had taken. I was in time to see a smaller shape come bounding out of the fog towards a bigger shape. A few more steps showed me mother and child re-united. The cow was standing still, broadside on to me and quite unconcerned about my presence, while a sleek three months' old calf was sucking away like anything at her udder. I stayed a minute, watching, because it was such a safe and peaceful sight. I envied that calf for having its mother all to itself and for the many long summer days the two of them must have spent roaming the moor together, always with plenty of food at hand, for Dartmoor has very good grazing for cattle and sheep throughout the summer.

Then I turned back towards the moor-gate, feeling very sad and puzzled as well as frightened now, because it was plain that since our cows were not even visible yet, I would have to give up trying to find them and just go home without them as quick as I could.

Even then I had no idea how much danger I was in. I walked fast and when after five minutes the moor-gate did not come into sight I began to run. I ran faster and faster until I was hot and gasping, then stopped and listened intently. There was nothing to hear but the wind howling and there was nothing to see except the fog.

I started crying then, but not my usual silent crying. It was the sort of noise I had never made before and certainly never have since. It was more like yelling. It has stayed with me throughout the whole of my life. Sometimes even now I waken from a dream, sweating with fear, and hear in my head the very same sounds I made on the moors that night when I suddenly knew that I was trapped, that the fog had really got me in its jaws.

To be in a panic is much the same as being out of your wits. You can make a lot of noise, you can cover a tremendous lot of ground, you can lose a lot of sweat and you can even do a lot of praying – but all to no purpose. What you are really doing is running away from something unbearable in your own mind. In the end you have to stop running away and look your trouble squarely in the face. What is more, you have to look closely and trace out the lines of that face. This is your main hope of getting back to safety.

Lots of people, very good and sensible people too, say that your main hope is to pray to God. That is all very well, but I think it depends what you pray to God *for*. If you ask him to alter things for you, to disperse the fog or stop the rain or bring daylight out of darkness, then you are still running away. Nothing in nature is ever going to be altered for you, you can be certain of that. But if you ask God for the courage and strength you'll need for coping with your trouble, then you'll probably get it. But you must have a plan of action first.

I must have been in a panic for quite a long time. Whether or not I did any praying I don't remember, probably I did, but I certainly remember doing lots of running in lots of different directions.

It was really the panic that caused all the trouble. There are two sensible things I could have done as soon as I made the discovery that the fog had swallowed me. One was, to guide myself by the direction of the wind. I already knew the wind was coming up out of the south-west, out of the low country towards Tavistock, and I knew also that that was the right direction for Sunset. If I had kept the wind in my face and gone on walking steadily I would certainly have come down off the high moors out of the fog. Perhaps I would have come down on to some other farm, but it would have been a simple matter to get from there to Sunset. The other thing I might have done was to go downhill until I found a stream. This would have been more difficult, because in a dense fog it's hard to tell whether you are going up or down or level. But once I had found a stream I would only need to follow it far enough and it would lead me off the moor, though it might very likely be in some place miles from home.

But my panic prevented me from doing either of those things. I just ran about on those moors crying and often stumbling over rocks. I fell down several times, cutting my hand once on a jagged rock. I saw it bleeding badly, but I never felt any pain from it. There was so much pain in my mind that I couldn't possibly feel it anywhere else. At times I stopped to listen, in case I might hear that cow again, but there was never any sound but the wind. If I could have found that cow and calf again I think I would have stayed with them, though it wouldn't have helped me at all. If it had been a wet summer I would have heard running water sooner or later, but after the weeks of sunshine all the streams had become trickles.

I longed to see a landmark I could recognize, even if it was only some rock with a special shape that Beth and I had often seen before when gathering cows or sheep on these moors. I thought I knew all this part of the moor so well, but now everything looked completely strange and different.

When at last I did come across something familiar and easily recognizable it was not a comfort after all, but a shock. It was the skeleton of a pony lying near what during most of the year was a bright green bog. It was not a bog now, though it was still much greener than anywhere else. As soon as I saw this I turned round and ran off in the opposite direction, not because I was afraid of the skeleton, which was well known to us all at Sunset, but because I knew it was not anywhere near the moor-gate. It was on a much higher and wilder part of the moor which we did not usually go to except after sheep. The remains of the pony told me that a lot of my running must have been directly away from the moor-gate. It was a shock, too, to be reminded of how that pony had died. Pa and Sam had discovered it one February day, not last winter but I think the one before, and had done everything they could to save it. We never did discover whom it belonged to. It had gone a bit too near the edge of the bog to reach some tempting green grass and had got its legs trapped. Pa and Sam had gone home for ropes and for another man from a neighbouring farm and then gone out to the moor again to drag it back on to firmer ground, but the pony was too exhausted and would not get up and fight for its life. It had probably been in the bog several days already when they found it and had had enough and wanted to die. Pa even went out again next day with a sackful of hay, but the pony wouldn't eat. That is the way animals die in Dartmoor bogs. They do not sink into them and drown, they get their legs trapped and die of exhaustion after struggling for days to get free. It was quite a big pony and the foxes and buzzards had not even finished picking its bones a whole month later, when Pa saw it.

I was not afraid of bogs, because I knew they were not dangerous to humans except after many weeks of rain, but I was horrified at finding myself on that part of the moor where the skeleton was. After all my running I was farther away from home than before I started. And what chance did I have of keeping in any one direction at all? I remembered a story I had read about a man lost in a great forest, in Canada it was I think, and in winter with snow on the ground. He walked for hours and at last to his great delight came upon fresh foot prints. When he had followed them for some time he noticed with a horrible shock that they were his own. Was this sort of thing going to happen to me?

Well, it was. That skeleton came into sight again, in what seemed to be quite a different direction and after what seemed to be an awfully long run.

It was exhaustion that made me sit down and begin to think and try really to face what I was up against. The daylight had been fading so gradually that I hadn't noticed it during the worst of my panic. But now I saw that it was much more than half gone, that it would be pitch-black night in a short time.

And then the first drops of rain started.

8. Where's Peter?

You will be wanting to know what was happening down at the farm during all this time of fading daylight. Well, even though I wasn't there, I can describe it all for you just as vividly as if I had been, because of the way Beth kept on talking to me about it for days afterwards, and not only Beth but Sam and the grown-ups too.

It was Granma in the farmhouse who first noticed something was wrong. Going about her work with all the doors and windows wide, she was keeping her ears on the alert for the first sounds of the cows coming into the yards. When they did so, it was her intention to go out and help me to get them into their stalls and tie them up.

As time lengthened and still they did not come, she went out into the yards to listen. No sounds of life or movement were coming from Little Mead, so she decided to go back up to Bullmeadow to tell them that there was no sign yet of either me or the cows. But first she went to the stable for a pony bridle, which she took with her. She found Ma and Beth busy on the stack while the others were some distance out in the field.

Only a few minutes ago Beth had said –

'Ma, I keep hearing Peter crying. D'you think I'd better go in case he's taken hurt some ways?'

'How *could* you hear him?' Ma had said sharply. 'He's 't other side of farm, for one thing – and for another, he's never one for cryin' out loud.'

'Oh, but I mean in my mind,' Beth had said, 'that's where I keep hearing 'im. I'm all fret up and scarey.'

'Wait till one more load's up,' Ma had replied. 'Maybe 't will be the last, or the next to it. I'll own I'm not easy in my mind about him myself.'

So when Granma arrived with her news, Beth and Ma looked at each other in alarm. Then Beth was down the ladder in no time at all, snatching the bridle out of Granma's hand and running off to the next field to catch Dong before anyone could either tell her to do so or stop her from doing it.

Granma gazed after her in amazement.

'Bless my soul, there's a child that knows her own mind an' goes her own wilful way.'

'You surely know what she is, Mother, where Peter's concerned. Like a hen with one chick.'

Granma climbed the ladder. She might be getting on in years, she might be tired out, but certainly she could not resist the desire to get up there on top of that lovely new stack, the fruit of all the labour and the sweat of that livelong day.

Jim's arrival with another load prevented the two women from having any further discussion about me. Ma was glad to have Granma to take Beth's place in shifting the hay round the stack. Not until Jim had finished pitching up that load was he invited to have his say about the situation. He guessed at once that the cows must have broken out and that I was still hunting for them somewhere.

'What have 'ee got next door to Little Mead?' he asked. 'You'm gettin' well up in the world, Missis – can't 'ee see the whole farm from up there?'

'There's Mid Mead on one side and the oats field on 't other,' said Ma.

'Ah, then I reckon that's where them cows 'o yourn be to. Up to their necks in the oats. 'Tis exactly the sort o' caper they'd get up to on a day the like o' this, with all of us up to our necks in hay.'

'But they're *not* in the oats,' said Ma. 'I can *see* the oats field.'

'Maybe they'm under the hedge, ye wouldn't see 'em then. Or lyin' down in it, with their bellies full – I doubt ye'd see 'em at all, in this light.'

'But Peter would have had 'em out of it by now, for certain.'

'Happen he's a bit small to shift 'em away from a treat like that.'

'Oh dear, oh dear,' said Ma. 'How many more loads, Jim?'

'Two, I reckon. But here come Maister now, he can tell 'ee better'n I.'

When he heard about my strange absence, the first thing Pa did was to go up on the stack and have a good look round the farm.

'They'm not in the oats,' he said, 'that's one good thing. Hey, where's our little maid flyin' off to?'

He had just seen Beth, now mounted on Dong, trotting off beyond the yards into the orchard. He was in a good humour because the next load, he told them, would be the last. If he was worried at all it was only because the cows must have broken out, not because I was missing.

'So we can manage without Beth now,' Ma said. 'A good thing too, for we'd have had to anyway – she thinks the boy must have taken some hurt and has gone off real headstrong to find him. She's been hearing things in her mind, you know the way she does – and I'm worried, John, I can tell 'ee. She's too often right.'

'One more load and then we'll see to it,' Pa said. 'Doant 'ee worry, I reckon that boy's a bit wore out, that's all. Sat down to rest his legs an' dropped off to sleep, that's about the shape of it.'

Granma went home and met the cows coming into the yards. She opened the shippen door and was starting to fasten their chains when Beth called from outside –

'Peter's on the moor and I'm going to find him before 'tis too late.'

Then she was off again and when Granma went out to call her back there was only the sound of her pony's hooves scrabbling upwards in a great hurry towards the Big Mead gateway.

Granma blessed her soul a good deal over that, but went back into the house to continue getting the evening meal. Then a few minutes later she came out again to start milking. The farm work had got to be done no matter what happened. Already there was hardly enough light to see what one was doing in the shippen.

The haymakers came noisily into the yard soon afterwards, talking and laughing, with a feeling of triumph for having completed the hard task they had set themselves. The last thing they had done was to spread a tarpaulin over the stack and tie it down securely.

Sam was given the job of unharnessing the horses while the others came into the shippen to milk. During a time like this it was a matter of course for everyone to milk, for there would be neither rest nor food for anyone until it was done. When the whole family set about it together, to say nothing of Jim, the ten cows could all be milked in a quarter of an hour.

When Pa heard Granma's account of how Beth had gone off to the moor, he said, seizing a bucket and sitting down under a cow –

'Well, I'm jiggered! What in thunder can be the matter with these chillern tonight? Have they lost their wits?'

Ma was sitting next to him.

'An' if they have, John, 'tis you overdrivin' 'em that's done it. So you can ease off blamin' 'em, else I'll be givin' 'ee some hard words myself, that I will.'

There was a silence then in the shippen except for the loud purring of milk streaming into buckets. Then Jim said, slowly and thoughtfully –

'Baint very healthy out on moor tonight, I doubt. They tops was all gone away into mist as I rode up from Tavy.'

A minute after this, Ma jumped up from her stool as if she had been stung by a wasp.

'Oh my dear lord,' she cried out, staring down at her husband in the half-darkness. 'That child's right, John, Beth's right, as usual. Peter never saw them cows standin' round Big Mead gate, wouldn't have seen 'em from where he was. An' he's out on the moor for sure, lookin' for cows that aint there.'

Pa just looked at her, going on milking, but thinking very hard. Then he called to Granma –

'Mother, are ye sure them cows came in through Big Mead gate?'

She said she *was* sure, so Pa got up, looking extremely grave.

'Then they broke into Mid Mead and the boy saw as how they'd have gone out to moor –'

'Yes, an' wouldn't know they'd come back,' Ma finished

for him. 'Oh my gracious me, John, he could get himself lost up there – nearly dark as 'tis.'

At that moment Sam came in to milk, saying cheerfully –

'Rain just settin' down proper, Pa. Caw, aint we been lucky, just!'

It was then they first began to realize they were faced with something big, big enough to make everyone forget even the cows for a while. If I was on the moor, with daylight all but gone, it was pretty certain I was lost.

Pa and Jim started off at once for the Big Mead, taking with them the two lanterns that were ready to be used in the shippen. It was agreed that Ma and Sam should follow as soon as they had equipped themselves with all the things they could think of that they might need – raincoats, more lanterns, spare candles for these, matches and a flask of brandy.

9. Beth at the Moor-gate

From all her descriptions of it afterwards, I know just what sort of state Beth was in about me ever since Granma appeared at the foot of the haystack. It wasn't only a frenzy of anxiety, it was also a bursting inner need to *do* something about me at once. Since she was the only one who knew that things had gone badly wrong with me, she felt it was up to her alone to go to my rescue.

As soon as she was astride of Dong, her tensions began to flow out of her into the pony through her legs and thighs which gripped and squeezed in all kinds of unusual motions. As for him, he had had a very boring day, just standing about flicking tails with Ding and Jamey, a swarm of flies round him and no interesting grass within miles because of the drought. Now he was ready to go anywhere and do anything, especially as the heat of the day had gone with the approach of darkness. When that pulsing human body began to play its silent language of crisis all over his back, he was in exactly the right mood to respond.

Beth had no difficulty in getting him into a canter at every opportunity and he behaved so well that she was able to open and close gates without dismounting. In the Little Mead she found at once the gap in the hedge that the cows had made and such was Dong's trust in her that he scrambled up and through without even stopping to examine it.

That brought her into Mid Mead, where she had to pull Dong tight to a stand-still so that she could decide which way to go. Then suddenly, like a flash of light in her mind, she saw, as I had done in that same field barely an hour ago, what that gap in the hedge really meant – that the cows had gone all the way out to the moors that day, just as they usually did. But she saw more than I had been able to. She saw also how likely it was that by this time they had come back on their own and were standing, silent and unnoticed by anyone, patiently waiting at the gate down at the bottom of Big Mead.

From Mid Mead through the open gate into Big Mead and then all the way down to the bottom of it Dong really went like a hare, for it was all downhill and there were drops of exciting rain in the wind. They arrived amongst the sleepy cows almost before these had had time to do more than turn their heads to see what all the noise and fuss was about.

Beth opened the gate for them, then counted them as they moved lazily through it. There was just enough light left for her to see that they were all there, including the bull. Then she paid her flying visit to the shippen, called out to Granma, and in no time at all was away again out of the yards and up through the length of Big Mead as if the devil were after her, pounding her knees into Dong's sides and smacking his flank with her bare hand.

Anyone watching would have judged that she was enjoying herself as much as her pony was. How could she help it, in spite of all her anxiety? The flying hedges in the twilight, the thudding hooves on the grass and the dust rising from Dong's scrabblings to get a foothold on the hard bare earth in the gateways – all this gave her a feeling as if she were playing the leading part in some famous story.

Dong kept up a fast pace all the way to the moor-gate, where he arrived blowing and snorting, very glad to have a rest. Beth dismounted and hitched his bridle to the gate post. She also was out of breath and had suddenly become very frightened. Beyond the moor-gate there was that curtain of fog, not grey any more as I had seen it, but dark, brownish, already almost part of the night. And the wind was strong and howling, with increasing spots of rain in it. She started calling at the top of her voice –

'Peeee-ter, Pee – ee – ee-ter,' and since the wind would carry the sound the way she wanted it to go there did seem to her a chance that I might hear. She sent out the call again and again, listening intently between calls and watching Dong's ears which were a comforting sight as they made fascinating twists and turns because of her calls. Then suddenly she screamed, because an animal was rubbing against her leg.

It was only Toby. She recognized him quickly enough to change the last bit of the scream into a laugh, then swung round quickly to see if someone else from the farm might be with him. There was no one else and she was half glad, in case someone might have heard that scream.

Toby had come from behind her, she was sure of that.

'Oh Toby,' she said, 'why did you leave Peter? Why did you, how *could* you – oh you bad dog, you bad dog!'

But she could not make her voice severe because he was nuzzling her hand and beating his tail against the back of her legs, very pleased to see her.

She never doubted for a moment that I was on the moor, not even now when she knew the cows were all down in the shippen being milked and so there was no longer any reason for my being out there at all. Ever since before leaving the hay field some secret place in her mind had been receiving distress messages about me. They were coming in now more strongly than ever, always from the same direction, tugging her away from the farm into the great dark emptiness of the fog and the night. Should she go farther? *Could* she go any farther?

'No, I can't' she said aloud. 'I can't, can I, Toby? I can't possibly be brave enough for that.'

The rain was increasing steadily. Even while she watched, the curtains she was facing became more and more like rain and less and less like fog.

She went back to calling 'Peee-ee-ter' and an owl screeched somewhere out in the murky darkness. It screeched again and this time the screech was moving. Then she was just able to see the owl float past across her line of vision, low down as if it had come to find out what all this calling could mean.

'Mr. Owl,' she cried out in sudden desperation, 'please go and find Peter – you can see in the dark – please go an' tell him I'm here.'

Another distant screech came from much farther away, beyond the curtain, so she could almost believe the owl had understood.

Now she was getting soaking wet and rather cold. After all the heat and sweat of the day this wet wind seemed to go right through her. She would just *have* to go home soon – or could she perhaps get shelter under Dong's fat comfortable tummy?

But now her whole mind was suddenly invaded more vividly than ever by thoughts of me somewhere out there in all that murk, without any warm solid pony to lean against, without any sheepdog nuzzling my hand. I, her special brother that she had played with every day ever since she could remember, was out there in that great emptiness, alone, lost, crying – perhaps frantic. It was unbearable to think about. I would be wet through by now, for certain, for I was only wearing shirt, trousers and boots. I was afraid of the dark and it would be dark in a few minutes now, really pitch-black dark. What on earth would I *do* if I were out there all night, what else had anyone ever thought it possible to do since the beginning of the world, except snuggle down deep in bed? And if there were no bed, no house, no Ma and Pa, no pony, no dog even – what then? It was almost unimaginable; almost, but not quite. Beth did imagine it, while both rain and tears ran steadily down her face.

'Oh Toby,' she said in surprise, 'I'm crying just like Peter does.'

This was so agonisingly painful, standing there thinking about me, that she became capable of almost anything that might have even a slight chance of ending it. Should she, could she, get up on Dong and go out over the moor, calling? She was back again trying to deal with that suggestion, or was it a temptation? Perhaps anything was better than staying there imagining the unbearable. Yes, she knew now she could find will-power enough to go out there over the moor, so as to put an end to this pain. But what good would it do if she were to get lost too? She knew that if some powerful magician came up to her now and offered her the chance to change places with me, she would accept eagerly. It could not be more painful for her to be out there, lost and frantic, perhaps all night, than it was for her standing there by the moor-gate.

'But then,' she thought aloud, 'if I do change places with

him, then *he* will have to stand here thinking about *me* and will he like that any better?'

That thought did her a lot of good. It seemed to release her from the unbearableness of her own imagination. Perhaps, she thought, I was having the best of it after all. For what did *she* have in store for her, if I did not come back? A night of torment in a warm bed? If you have to endure a night of torment, does it matter all that much whether you are in bed or battling with rain and wind on the moor?

All this pain then, she realized, was because she loved me so much, because I was part of her, because anything that I felt and thought she also had to think and feel. How strange, that just loving someone could cause one so much pain. But probably I did not love her as much as she did me, because I did not have what she had heard Ma and Granma say that she had, the mothering urge. No, of course as a boy I couldn't have that.

She felt it was impossible to go home, even now that she was wet through and thoroughly chilled. For what would home be without me? Well, there were her parents, and Sam, and her grandparents, and her kitten, and her pet calf. Were they not enough for one eleven-year-old girl? Could she not go on living quite nicely without me at all? No – oh no, most certainly not, because without me there would be no one to speak to without words, no one to tell her special private secrets to. But then Sam, she felt sure, did not have anyone to share his life with and he seemed to enjoy it quite as much as she and I, if not more so. Perhaps, then, it was not part of ordinary everyday life, to have someone you loved as much as she loved me, perhaps it was something added on to everday life that you had to pay for with extra pain?

All these thoughts went flashing through her as she stood

there calling to me, some of them familiar but several of them altogether new ones for her. There was something about her position there, on the edge of nothingness, that forced her to think deep and far. She had never before considered the possibility of my dying, but now she had to. What would become of her if I did? And, more important still, what would become of *me*? There were plenty of grave-stones in Martha Tavy churchyard which said children were lying under them, some of them about my age. Where had they gone to, really? If they had gone to heaven, did they go on growing up there? Probably they did not, because if they did they would have to stop growing sometime and that would mean dying over again. So if I went to heaven I would stay always the same age as I was now and so would never become a real artist. That she found a very comforting thought, for Miss Scrimshaw had said God wanted me to be an artist, which must mean that God did not want me to die.

The rain was very heavy now and she must have crouched down underneath Dong's tummy without even knowing she was doing it, for that was where she found herself when she came out of her long trails of thought and heard Pa calling her name somewhere in the fields behind and below. She called out as loud a reply as she could, but stayed where she was because it was now too dark to move and she was a bit scared in case Dong might step on her by mistake. In a minute she saw the lights of two candle lanterns coming towards her and then saw Pa and Jim with the other sheep-dog at their heels.

'Now God be thanked here's one of 'em safe and sound,' Pa said as he reached her and held the lantern high to get a view of her and the pony and Toby.

He put out an arm and pulled her against him, saying –

'Brave little maid you be, Beth, and no mistake,' with the result that she burst out crying in her usual way, at the top of her voice and mouth wide open, so that she could not hear the next words he said and Jim only just caught them.

The next thing she knew was, she had been lifted on to Dong by Jim, who then, with the lantern in one hand and Dong's bridle in the other, started leading her down towards home.

Pa called after them – 'Hand her over to the wife and come back up, I'll be wantin' 'ee bad.'

Left alone, the first thing Pa did was to send his voice out over the moors in a long-drawn-out Hullo-o-o. It was a voice trained by long practice in shouting instructions to dogs gathering sheep on far hillsides. But in such a storm of wind and rain as was breaking over Dartmoor now, he did not feel much confidence in it.

So the second thing he did was to call the names of his two dogs, wave his arm at the moors and shout – 'Git up around! Git up around!' They went off into the night like sprinters at a starting gun, yelping with excitement. He knew they would make for the high ground in search of sheep and circle far, barking as they went. There was just a chance, Pa thought, that the commotion they would make might attract my attention better than his calling, if I were still anywhere on the home moors.

In spite of the darkness, the dogs might bring sheep and cattle running down to him with his lantern at the moor-gate, so the third thing he did was to shut this gate, blaming himself bitterly as he did so for having allowed the family to get into the habit in mid-summer of leaving it open. To shut it when bringing the cows in off the moor in the evenings would mean that someone would have to toil up through the fields to open it again after milking next morning. It was only too plain to him now that cutting out this little bit of work, so as to gain a little more precious hay-making time, had been the main cause of this trouble that had come upon them.

10. Gone to Earth

I needed cooling down after all that running and the rain certainly did that for me. Although I knew it was the most serious thing of all, the rain did not increase my panic, it did just the opposite. I suppose that was because I knew that I had now reached the worst, that things could not possibly go more wrong than they had gone now. The coming of the rain meant that, besides all the misery and fear of being lost, there was a possibility of actually dying on the moor. My panic went away, quite suddenly, because now I knew I would have to fight for my life. I would have to have a cool mind, therefore, and think really straight, because otherwise there might be no Peter Varden any more, no more farmer's son and no more artist, there would be nothing at all, just an empty space like this fog. If everything depended on *me*, then I could be stronger and braver and more sensible than I had ever been in my life before. I had no choice. It was either that or the end.

You see, I was having my first glimpse of that awkward bit of truth that you have to discover for yourself at some stage during your growing-up, I mean the knowledge that death may come at any time even for *you*, whether your name is Peter Varden or John Smith, Beth Varden or Mary

Smith, and that if it does come and take you away it will take away your whole world as well – because if you are not there to see and feel it any more, it has gone, hasn't it, as far as you are concerned?

So I stood up straight, with that cool rain coming down on my hot face, and said loud and clear in a steady voice –

'Now I've got to find shelter, that's all. Remember what Pa said.'

He had said it last year, to Sam, who had been out on the moor with the Narracott boys, had got caught in the rain and had come home at dusk looking like a drowned rat.

'Doant 'ee ever get overtook by dark an' rain together, boy, on they old moors. 'Tis a likely death for a strong man, to be wanderin' all night up there in streams o' rain and a cruel wind. A roof over your head an' a bit o' shelter, that's what'll save 'ee, even if 'tis no more than a slab of granite under one of they old tors. So you *mind* that, see? Better to crouch all night in a hole and stay livin', than to keep searchin' your way home an' have all the spirit ravaged out of 'ee on the bare moor.'

Yes, I could hear Pa's voice saying it, at tea time that day last year, a Sunday in October I think it was. He said it to Sam but he meant it for all three of us because he used the special deep tone that he kept for important things. Sam was stuffing food inside him and looking peculiar, not because he had taken any harm from getting soaked, but because his hair had not been so clean for months and he was wearing one of Pa's jerseys.

It helped a lot to listen to Pa's voice, even though it was only in my mind. I started running again, though not fast, just a steady jog-trot and this time I tried to keep uphill because I was thinking of all those jumbled rocks which composed Raven's Tor, the first big tor you came to on our part of the moor. There would surely be a chance of shelter there if only I could find it. I had sense enough now to keep the wind behind me so as to be sure I was going in one direction all the time.

The rain was getting thicker and the wind much stronger, blowing the fog away but not helping because the curtains of rain were just as blinding. I could tell by now that it was going to be one of those tearing, raging nights when the rain comes against the windows as if someone is throwing it in buckets and the wind breaks trees and knocks down chimney-pots. I was wet through already, I could feel the water running down my neck, but I was still warm. I even wondered for a few minutes if I might be able to keep running all night and so prevent myself from ever getting cold enough to have 'my spirit ravaged out of me'. But really I knew there wasn't any hope of that.

It was just about then that I heard an owl screeching. It was the first sound I had heard, except for the wind, since that cow and calf, so I stopped at once to listen and had another thought. Where there were owls there were usually trees. So when the screech came once more from the same place I changed my direction and started running again. Very soon the running became so much easier than I knew I must be going downhill.

The ground got steeper and rougher, slowing me down to a walk and then to a very slow scrambling gait, because great rocks and bushes and brambles were getting in my way. I kept falling and probably hurting myself, but I didn't care. I was like a rabbit running for cover into a hedge or a wood. My idea now was that the rougher and steeper the ground became the more likely I was to find trees or rocks or caves or at least something that would let me get out of the rain. The owl still let out a screech now and then, or perhaps there were two of them answering each other, so I was able to keep on in the same direction.

Then I came to something so steep that it was more like a bank which I was slithering down, unable to stop. When I got to my feet again at the bottom I heard what sounded like trees tossing in the wind. It was nearly dark now, but when I looked carefully I could just see smallish trees growing amongst huge boulders and rocks. It was just the sort of place I wanted. I started to hunt then, groping my way carefully around clumps of brambles and great gorse bushes that tore at my face and hands. I was hunting for a cave or a hole or an overhanging slab of stone, just as a wild animal might do, straining my eyes like anything to use every bit of light there was left.

I climbed up a great mound of what seemed like bare earth, and at the top, at one side under some overhanging gorse bushes, was a hole. Being on my hands and knees I noticed at once that the loose earth all round the hole was dry, quite dry and powdery. So I put my head down and looked into the hole. It went sideways into very steep ground above. When I tried it with my arm the arm went in up to my shoulder and my hand felt soft dry leaves on the floor of the hole. There was a strong animal smell coming out. I knew it must be a fox's or badger's earth and that I couldn't have found anything better.

I twisted myself round, lay down on my tummy and shoved my legs backwards into the hole. They went in as far as my hips, then stuck for a moment, but more pushing with my hands sent them farther down until my shoulders stuck. Another strong push put me in altogether, leaving only my head sticking out because that didn't want to go under yet. It was a very strange feeling. I had gone to earth like a rabbit or a fox. I really knew for a few minutes what an animal that lives under the ground feels like when it gets back home underneath after facing all sorts of dangers in the world above. I had gone back hundreds of thousands of years.

It was only for a few minutes, though, because a whole bookful of thoughts came flowing into my mind about my real home and how far away and out of reach it seemed and how many long hours of darkness there would have to be before I could get back to it. I thought about all the family and the hay and whether they had managed to finish the field before the rain and what they had done and said when they came down to the yards and found no cows and no Peter. I wondered which of them would be the most upset about me and decided that of course it would be Beth and the next most would be Ma. Pa wouldn't worry at all at first, he would say I had probably dropped off to sleep, because that was the sort of thing Sam had done sometimes when he was my age and Pa never seemed to notice that I wasn't really a bit like Sam.

I thought, too, about the cows and where in the world they could be, for I still hadn't managed to work out the explanation, that of course they had been waiting all the time at the bottom of Big Mead and perhaps were even still waiting there now in the darkness and the rain.

I also thought about the night that was coming, about the pelting rain that I could hear but not feel and the wind fairly screaming now in the trees above me. Would Beth be able to sleep tonight, thinking of me out on the moor in a tempest like this? Of course she would not. I pictured her lying in bed wide awake and I pictured my own empty bed in the next room. Would I ever get back where I belonged?

By this time my day had lasted over seventeen hours, for it must have been well after ten o'clock and the last glimmer of daylight had gone. I was beginning to forget how cold and miserable and lost I was, I was beginning to forget even how to remember my whole world of Sunset Farm, it was all drifting away into nothingness, into fog, into sleep, into dreams.

11. Dreaming

It started with Beth and me out on the moor picking wortleberries, as we did every summer after haymaking. Some of the best worts were in the neighbourhood of the bog with the skeleton beside it. When we came to the skeleton we found it was not a skeleton at all but a grey pony with a long thin nose and dreamy misty eyes. It looked fairly comfortable, lying there with its legs out of sight in the bog and its head raised up to look at us with a languid interest.

'Hullo, Mrs. Pony,' I said.

Beth said to me – 'Yes, but *how* do we know it's a Mrs?'

I did not answer her because the pony had started to speak.

'Hullo, you Varden children. I've often seen you on the moor.'

Then Beth asked the pony if she wanted our help to get out of the bog.

'No, thank you, children,' the pony replied. 'I'm really very comfortable and my time has come for dying. The Queen will look after me.'

'What Queen?' I asked.

'The Queen of Dartmoor, of course. She is going to eat me,

which is really quite fair because I've been eating her all my life and I've lived a long time.'

'Won't it hurt?' Beth asked.

The pony shook her head. 'Not if I'm ready. But I don't want them to start till I'm ready, that is *not* fair. Perhaps you can help me over that.'

'Who do you mean by "them"?' Beth asked.

'I mean the wolves,' said the pony. 'They are the worst. Then there are the foxes and the ravens and the buzzards, but they are usually well-behaved and don't start eating you until you are really dead.'

'But there *aren't* any wolves!' Beth and I said, both at the same time.

The pony nodded her head and looked beyond us into the distance. 'You say that because you don't live on the moor. You only come here occasionally and in daytime. You have to live on the moor to know what really goes on here. If you listen hard you can sometimes even hear the wolves in broad daylight. Listen!'

We both listened carefully and there *was* a distant howling, rather like the Mary Tavy mine siren, but going up and down in waves. It seemed to be coming from underground.

'There you are,' said the pony. 'That means they'll probably come out tonight or tomorrow night, which is hard luck for me because at this rate I shall need another two days at least to die comfortably. They only come out about once a month, usually on dark and stormy nights. Then they go streaming across the higher moors in a long line behind their leader, a thing you never forget once you've seen and heard it. Their leader is called Grark and is very well educated and speaks several languages. It is said he was once a man but got changed into a wolf for committing some awful crime. I've spoken to him once or twice – only that was when I was younger and had one of my foals with me. The wolf pack usually goes after sheep, and leaves us ponies alone because we know how to fight with our hooves. But they eat us pretty quick when we're dead – or dying.'

'But the Queen,' I said, 'didn't you say it was the Queen who was going to eat you?'

'Oh, you don't understand,' said the pony in a rather superior way, 'the Queen does not do her own eating, it's all done for her by her servants. And some of them get a bit out of control sometimes and eat when they shouldn't.'

We asked her again why she wanted to die and she said she was old, twenty years old, and very tired and she was sure she would never have another foal. The stallions were not interested in her any more. So what was there left to live for? Ever since the men had taken her last foal away from her she had been lonely and bored. The men must have sent her back on to the moor for no other reason than to let her die. She had been eating the moor for twenty years and now it was time for the moor to start eating her. That was how the system worked and she had no quarrel with it, so long as the eating did not start too soon.

When Beth asked what we could do to help her about this, she said –

'You can go and see the Queen and tell her about me and ask her not to let the wolves out during the next few days. She probably doesn't know about me, but I expect the wolves do.'

When we asked her how to find the Queen, she said casually –

'Oh, just go to the palace. Anyone will tell you where that is, even the rabbits know.'

Then everything changed. Beth disappeared and I went off alone to find the Queen. The first person I met to ask the way from was the big black cow with her calf. She looked at me doubtfully.

'You aren't old enough to go to the Queen, you aren't old enough to be out on the moor alone at all. You had better run off home as fast as you can.'

I said – 'Oh, so you don't know the way to the Queen? That's funny, the old grey pony said everyone knew that, even the rabbits.'

I was very surprised to find myself so cheeky and clever.

'Of course I know,' said the black cow. 'You must go to Raven's Tor and knock on the door.'

So I went straight to Raven's Tor, which is easy to find because you can see it for miles, and I found there *was* a door there, a huge door of solid granite. Since there was no knocker and I had nothing to knock with, I picked up a rock about the size of a loaf of bread and threw it at the door. It started opening very slowly, groaning as if its hinges needed oiling terribly badly. I went through as soon as there was room enough and found a stone staircase going down. After I had gone down three or four steps there was a heavy thud behind me and I saw over my shoulder that the door had closed. I went on down, not much afraid because I was excited and there was plenty of light coming through windows high up. At the bottom of the stairs was a broad level passage. After another minute of walking I came to a sort of hall with several passages leading out of it, all looking alike. I chose one of them and went on until it led into a long shed with stalls like a shippen. It was exactly like the Sunset Farm shippen, with the same number of stalls. There were walking breathing noises coming towards me from the other end of this long shed, as if creatures of some kind were about to enter it from the opposite passage. As I watched they did enter and took their places in the stalls like cows.

There were ten of them and they were all wolves, not very big ones, not much bigger than Toby, with long lean tawny bodies. They had taken no notice of me, so I thought I could turn round quietly and slip away without being seen. But in the passage I had come from was now standing another wolf, much bigger and all black, looking at me with his lips drawn back and his teeth showing.

I knew that if I tried to run away he would be after me in a flash and tear me to pieces. In any case, there was nowhere to run to except back into the wolves' shippen. So I just stood looking at him, pretending not to be afraid, until I had a sudden idea.

'Are you Grark?' I asked, trying to make my voice polite and interested.

He stopped curling his lips and said, in a very grand manner –

'I am Captain Grark, of the Queen's Guard. What do you want?'

'I want to see the Queen.'

'That's cheeky – ha-ha – you must be very young. Don't you know that nobody sees the Queen? Not even us, her life-guards. We only see her skirts. Who do you think you are? Are you of any importance?'

'I'm Peter Varden, of Sunset Farm, and I'm an artist – at least Miss Scrimshaw says I'm an artist.'

'To the devil with Miss Scrimshaw. I'll soon see if you're an artist. Come with me.'

There was something very imperious about him. He was evidently accustomed to being obeyed at once.

He took me down another passage into a kind of stone-walled room where there was a blackboard and some chalks. Then he went over close to the wall, struck an attitude as if he were going to be photographed, and said –

'Draw a picture of *me* and if you can do *that* then perhaps I'll see what I can do for you about the Queen.'

I took a good look at him, a better look than I had managed until now, because I had got over some of my fear. He held himself very stiffly, with his head up and staring straight before him, reminding me of a picture I had seen recently at school of a soldier standing to attention.

All I did was to look at that picture in my mind and then draw it on the board. It was easy. The thing was done in two minutes.

When I put down the chalk he came round to my side of the blackboard, took one look and sat down.

'Very good,' he said. 'And now write "Captain Grark" underneath it in large letters.'

When I had done that he said –

'Call me Captain Grark next time you address me. You are a very clever boy. You know how to get on the right side of the boss.'

He just sat there looking at the drawing for quite a long while, then he got up quickly, saying –

'I must bring my wives to see this,' and went out.

He brought them all in, all those wolves I had seen go into the stalls. He spoke to them in barks and growls, making them all sit down to look at that soldier on the blackboard. They were very docile and seemed impressed by it, but took hardly any notice of me. After a few minutes he ordered them all out again, and I suppose they must have gone back into their stalls.

Grark said –

'That was the Queen's milking herd that you've just seen. No human eyes have ever seen them before, do you know that? You can come and do some milking now – come along.'

So I had to sit on a stool in that shippen and milk those she-wolves. They had udders just like cows, only much smaller, and it was easy since they did not give much milk. Grark walked up and down beside me. When I asked him who usually milked them he said rather curtly –

'They have cubs, of course,' as if that explained everything.

When that was over I had two buckets of milk, if it could be called milk. It was the colour of wortleberry juice and my hands were all stained purple with it.

'Take that milk and we'll go and see something of the Queen,' said Grark. 'It may please her, perhaps. Wortleberries and cream is the only food she's ever been known to take.'

We had to go up a long, long stone staircase. Every now and then I had to put down the buckets to give my arms a rest. When I did this Grark looked fierce and ran up and down several steps impatiently. He was a horribly nervy sort of wolf.

At last we came out on to a terrace or platform and facing us was a rising slope of deep purple colour, with sunlight flooding upon it from a cloudless sky. The purple stuff was dazzlingly clear and yet at the same time soft and thick like a young sheep's fleece. It moved, too, in ripples and waves like a field of green corn or a drowsy summer sea. I had never seen anything like it in my life. I could only stare and stare, with my mouth open. But as I lifted my eyes higher I saw that the upper parts of this enormous purple slope were veiled in mist. The sky was not cloudless after all. There was just this one cloud that seemed to be joined to the purple slope.

'Skirts, that's all we ever see,' said Grark in a cross,

disappointed voice. 'Unless *you* can see more. You're the first human that's ever seen this at all.'

'But what's all that purple stuff the skirts are made of?' I asked.

'If you're an artist you ought to see better than me, but to my eyes it looks like heather.'

'So the Queen's – a sort of mountain? And I wanted to speak to her.'

I was disappointed and yet immensely impressed at the same time.

'Speak to the Queen?' Grark laughed. His laugh was not pleasant at all, it was bitter and scornful. 'Ha-ha – stuff and nonsense. Now empty those buckets, that's about the best we can do for her.'

'Empty them?'

'That's what I said. Sling the milk out of them as far as you can on to her skirts.'

I did as he told me. It was impossible not to do as he told you. We both watched as the purple milk sprayed out over the purple heather.

'Now follow me,' he said, going off down the steps.

I began thinking of home, so I stopped to look out of a window and saw a wide stretch of moor that seemed familiar. As I paused there I heard Pa's voice calling me from far away in the direction of the moor-gate. It sounded very urgent and I knew I must go home at once.

When we got down into what looked like one of the stone corridors near the wolves' shippen I told Grark that I was going home and started off in what I thought was the right direction. He gave me that horrible laugh again.

'Ha-ha – stuff and nonsense. There'll be no going home for you, my lad, not after all you've seen that humans aren't supposed to see at all. We shall keep you here and turn you into a wolf and you can come out hunting with us on stormy nights.'

He had got between me and the way I wanted to go. There was an open window close beside us.

'But listen,' I said, pointing to the open window, 'that's my father calling. Can't you hear? It's urgent.'

He poked his nose out of the window and as he did so I slipped past him and fled for my life down the corridor. I could hear him coming behind me but I dared not look back. I took a corridor that suddenly opened on the right and then the next one on the left and stopped dead just round the corner, not making a sound. I heard Grark's pattering feet go past the entrance and die away in the distance.

But how was I going to get out of those endless corridors? I followed the one I was in and came out suddenly in the wolves' shippen once more. All those she-wolf heads turned to look at me, but luckily they were all tied up and I was able to back out and sprint off again down the passage.

This time I was lucky. I somehow got into the right corridor, the one with the stone door at the end of it. As I raced for that door I heard Grark's feet again, coming nearer. How was I going to knock on the door? There were no big loose stones lying around on this side of it. When I reached it I kicked it hard with my boot, hurting myself badly, but it began to open. At that moment Grark came into sight, racing towards me at top speed. Was I going to be in time to squeeze through? I had one leg through when I felt Grark's teeth grab hold of the back of my trousers. Then I was down on the ground on my tummy with him on top of me and I gave a great yell. I heard it echoing down many stone corridors and then – I woke up and found an animal snuffling with a wet nose at my face. I let out a great yell, the loudest sound I have ever made in my life and then lay still, absolutely stiff with fright, listening to those two yells which I knew were really one and the same.

There was another noise, too, a scattering, pattering noise below me that could mean only one thing – a fair-sized animal was departing in a great hurry over loose earth and stones. I had hidden my face in my arms to protect myself from that animal. When I had recovered enough from my fright to be able to move my arms I saw that it was still black night, though it was just possible to distinguish earth from sky – or rather, earth from rain, for my ears told me that the rain was still coming down in sheets.

But I was dry and moderately warm. I knew I had been to sleep, perhaps for a long time, and had been awakened by an animal sniffing at my face – not Grark, but most probably brock, which was what we called a badger. Poor brock, coming back early after a night's hunting spoiled by rain and finding the entrance to his home occupied by this extraordinary and probably dangerous human animal, and then having that loud yell let off in his face! He must have been for a few moments the most terrified badger in the world. No wonder he made such a noise running away.

What a relief it was to me, to think about that badger and to know that there was something else in the world as frightened as I was. It made it possible for me to go off to sleep again. There really was not anything else to do.

12. Wet Morning

It was around midnight when the four of them, Pa, Ma, Sam and Jim, returned from the moor defeated. It was after they had managed to meet at the moor-gate for discussion and had learned that their supply of candles was used up. Without light there was nothing more they could do, except probably get lost themselves. So reluctantly they had to call off the search and use their last stub of candle to get them back again to the farm. Jim decided to go off home without coming to the house, for he was afraid his wife might think he had been injured in the mine if he stayed away from home any longer. But he had promised to raise the alarm in the village early in the morning.

It was very rare for the Varden family to have such bad moments as they did then. Beth, luckily for her, was out of it as much as I was, for in spite of what she had expected she had dropped asleep as soon as she lay down. Coming into the house made the three of them realize just how incredibly wet they were. The water was running off them into pools on the floor, so there was only one possible thing to do – strip off their sodden clothes in the scullery before going on into the warm kitchen.

The grandparents, who had been dozing in chairs by the

fire, roused themselves hastily and came out to hear the news, or rather the lack of it. Then Granma could not help expressing her shock at seeing so much bare flesh. In those days nakedness was supposed to be almost as bad as wickedness.

'God bless my suffering soul, 'tis a mercy Jim's not here to see you all mother-naked or next thing to it!'

Pa must have been at that moment about as miserable a man as it is possible to be. Besides the failure to find me he was now faced with another thing that he had been dreading for the last three hours. There would have to be a search-party organized tomorrow (no, not tomorrow but later that same morning), which would mean that everyone in the whole neighbourhood would be talking of how the Vardens had sent their youngest child to fetch cows off the moor at dusk and would be saying that he, John Varden, must therefore be a hard man who for the sake of a bit of extra hay would be careless of his children's welfare.

So when Granma made her foolish mistake (and it must be remembered that she was every bit as tired and worried as everyone else, except Sam who never worried), Pa turned on her with real anger in his voice.

'Doant 'ee stand there gawpin', Muther, git summat to cover us with – and make 'aste about it.'

Then when they came in to the fire with towels draped round them, Granpa had to go and make things worse by saying –

'That there moor-gate never should 'a bin leff open, that's where us ha' gone wrong. If I've said it once I've –'

'Ay, *said* it, like enuff,' interrupted Pa in a growling threatening tone, 'said it a thousand times maybe an' never once walked up there to shut 'un, did ye now? Doant 'ee start talkin' to me about laziness.'

All over that usually peaceful kitchen angry words were smouldering. I've always been glad I wasn't there to feel them, and that Beth wasn't either. Sunset farmhouse during that midnight hour was about as far from its placid self as it had ever been in all its three hundred years.

Sam was too busy eating to bother with what the adults were saying, Ma was dumb with exhaustion and with the effort of drying her hair. Nevertheless it was she who intervened to soothe away the anger and bitterness. She decided that this was the time for that bottle of brandy which she had for many years kept in store for emergencies.

A stiff drink for all of them made it possible for them all to be asleep a quarter of an hour later, with a plan of action for tomorrow already sketched out. That is one thing to be said for long hours of hard manual labour – they make it not only possible but certain that sleep will soon come to the rescue of people suffering from even the most piercing anxieties.

Granma was the first up in the morning. She went down very silently, stoked up the fire, examined and shifted the drying boots, then opened the outside door. There was a grey promise of daylight, but the rain was still coming down heavily through a gusty wind. Out in the yards there was no sound of life except running water, no cock-crow, no bird-song, no young calves calling for milk, no pigs snorting. Such excessive rain had hushed all living things.

She thought she had moved so quietly, but Beth had heard and came down to join her.

'Get you some milk, child,' Granma said in a whisper. 'You look famished. And doant 'ee fret so. 'Tis middlin' warm an' maybe he's taken no great harm. Now daylight's coming he'll soon be found.'

'When can I go out to moor again, Granma? An' why

for's everyone sleepin' still? Shall I go an' rouse 'em out?'

'No, child, let 'em bide till there's a bit more light and do 'ee come and help me get some bacon fryin'. Summat to hearten their insides, that's what they'll be needin' with a day like this before 'em.'

'I dreamed he was lost in a girt hay-mow, Granma. We was all pullin' an' pullin' at the hay with our bare hands, tearin' it out in bits 'cause he was down inside suffocatin' and we dursent use prongs for fear o' stickin' 'im. Ooh, 't was awful–'

'Now then, me dear, we've enough to do without clobbering our minds with the like o' that – Git that table laid.'

'How soon can I go out to moor again?'

'Your Pa'll have to tell 'ee that. Sam's going over to Bodsworthy first thing, to get those two lads o' theirs that know the moor so well – so maybe you can be going out with them, but if 't were me to decide I'd say ye'd best stay home today, Beth.'

'Oh, *no* – I can't – I *can't* keep thinking of him out there an' not go. What's he doing out there now, Granma, what's he really a-*doing* of, do 'ee think?'

'That boy's got sense enough to be sleepin' somewheres, that's what *I* think.'

Beth was allowed to go and wake the others as soon as the smell of frying bacon began to pervade the house. When the grandfather clock struck four they were all sitting at breakfast, with a lamp on the table, but with enough daylight outside for them to see across the yard.

The plan they agreed on was for Pa to go out to the moor at once, alone and on foot, to be followed later by Ma and Beth, and for Sam to fetch his pony and go over at once to Bodsworthy to get as much help from there as was possible. Granpa would go down towards the village to meet the search-party that they expected would soon be setting out from there as a result of Jim's efforts. Beth at first wanted to go off at once with Pa, but had to be dissuaded, for he intended to do his fastest pace which she would have no chance of keeping up with. He would be going into places where no pony could venture.

'There'll be no fog, that's sure,' he said, putting on his half-dried boots, 'not after all this wind. I'm takin' both dogs an' if I don't find him in a couple of hours then he's gone off our moors altogether.'

He spoke as if one man and two dogs, if that man were himself, were all that could possibly be needed to search all the nearer moors. He was off a minute later, striding through the yards and calling to his dogs at the same time, secretly glad to be alone with his troubles. His hope was to bring me home before the search-party could be organized, before the whole countryside began to hum with the news of the boy lost on the moor.

Sam was off, too, a minute later, telling Beth he would bring in both ponies and leave Dong in the stable in case she might want him. Only Ma and Granma gave a thought to the cows, and to the calves and pigs that would soon be calling for their food.

'They'll just have to wait, that's all,' Ma said, but looked hopefully at Granma, who responded by saying that she would see what she could do later on.

Finally, Ma and Beth set out together for the moor, Granpa went off down the lane towards the village and Granma was left in sole charge of the farm. The first thing she did was to open a drawer in the dresser, take out the Bible and sit down at the table to read.

The rain poured down relentlessly outside and it was still only about five o'clock.

Being a very tough and hardy boy, both in mind and body, Sam was almost his usual happy-go-lucky self as he splashed his way along the already puddled track to Bodsworthy. He had not bothered to use his imagination and think of what might have been happening in my mind. Sam thought a lot of unnecessary fuss was being made. If I had been such a silly goat as to go into the fog, then of course I had got to pay the penalty, but why should a night's rain do me much harm, why did all the family have to get into such a steaming stew about it?

He was not worried either about the immediate job he had in front of him, which would be very hard for a timid or nervous boy. The Narracotts of Bodsworthy would all be enjoying a lie-in because of the rain, probably the first one they had had for weeks, and would not take kindly to being disturbed. They were a tough, rough family too, the Narracotts were. The two sons of fourteen and sixteen had a reputation for wildness. A year or two ago when they had both been of school age they had been notorious as the naughtiest boys in Martha Tavy.

As he rode into Bodsworthy farmyard three dogs came racing out and started barking savagely round Ding's heels. He had to shout at them in his best imitation of a full-grown farmer's voice to make them calm down enough to let him dismount and tie up the pony. Then, looking behind him in case he might have to boot one of the dogs, he went up to the back door and hammered on it with his fist. He was not embarrassed by causing all this sudden commotion in a sleeping farm. He thought it rather fun.

A window opened above him and a woman's face looked out, accompanied by a cross, sleepy voice.

'What's amiss, then, draggin' folk out o' their beds on such a day as this?'

''Tis a 'mergency, Missis,' Sam called up. 'Peter's lost on moor an' Pa says, could 'ee help us find 'im?'

The face disappeared and was replaced by a bearded man's.

'What the devil be any Varden doing on moor at this hour, boy?'

'He went to fetch the cows an' lost his way in fog.'

There was a mutter of talk from above, then the man called down –

'Doant make much sense to me. What in hell's name be Sunset cows doing on moor in rain an' storm the like o' this?'

Another window opened and a boy's voice called out –

'What's up, Sam? Be gettin' a good wash, b'aint 'ee?'

Sam was getting a trifle impatient.

'Naw, they cows weren't up there 'tall, only Peter thought they was. 'Twas last night –'

'*Last night?* Did 'ee say last night?' The man's voice had a different tone.

'Ay,' said Sam, 'we was all in a mortal hurry savin' hay an' Peter went for cows an' never came back.'

There was more talk upstairs, then the woman's head came out again alongside the man's.

'Be you sayin' your youngest's bin out on moor through all this night agone?'

'Ay, Missis,' Sam called back, 'that's how 'tis.'

'Godstrewth,' the man's voice said, 'then we've got to stir, me dear, like it or no.'

Instead of being let into the house Sam had instructions shouted down at him from the window – he was to go and fetch in the Narracott sons' two ponies while they got dressed and had a bite to eat. But once the household had become fully roused it was willing to treat Sam more kindly.

When he returned with the ponies he was invited in out of the rain and made to tell the whole story. The Narracotts had been famous moormen for generations. Anything that concerned the moor interested them at once and the thought of me wandering about lost up there in pouring rain became more of a challenge to them the more they thought about it. The two growing lads had ever since leaving school found their greatest enjoyment in life in hunting. They would hunt almost anything that lived on the moor, whether it was rabbits, hares, badgers, foxes or deer. Now they were being offered the chance of going hunting for a real live boy.

So they were soon ready to set off with Sam, leaving their father to come later on foot. Like my own father, he knew that a thorough search of the moors would mean going to places where a pony would be more of a hindrance than a help.

Meanwhile, Granpa was walking down to Martha Tavy, keeping reasonably dry in a long oilskin coat and hat. When he reached Jim's cottage he found Jim's wife already busy with the day's work, but no Jim. She said he had gone to the schoolmaster's house to give the news about my being lost and to get advice on what should be done. They had both agreed that Mr Dodd would be the best man to go to first. Although he was not a moorman at all and had only been a year or two in the village, he was the sort of man who always knew what to do when anything went wrong.

So Granpa went on to Mr Dodd's. There he found only Mrs Dodd, who was very sympathetic, asked him in for a cup of tea and told him her husband and Jim were busy waking up the most useful sort of men in other houses and that it would not be long before a proper search-party would be organized.

Granpa went on through the village and found two or

three men at the door of the Post Office, which was open, a very unusual thing for that hour of the morning. One of them recognized him and they gathered round him asking questions. This was his opportunity to explain how I had gone out on to the moor without anyone knowing, for he was as well aware as Pa that the Varden family would be blamed for allowing a child of my age to be out on the moor alone.

While they were talking, Mr Dodd came out of the Post Office and started fixing to the door a big sheet of paper which said

WANTED AT ONCE
VOLUNTEERS FOR SEARCH-PARTY
Peter, youngest child of Mr and Mrs Varden, of Sunset Farm, has been *LOST ON THE MOOR* since nine last night
MEET HERE, 7.30 this morning, Fri., 22 July

Mr Dodd also recognized Granpa, who had to give his explanation over again. There was then a discussion as to the best route to take in order to reach the moors above Sunset Farm. It was agreed that it would be best not to take the road to Sunset itself but to use another road out of Martha Tavy which would be more direct. One or two of the men present said they would start at once, but Mr Dodd decided that he would wait until seven-thirty and fill in the time until then by going round to some more houses in the village.

13. Nearly Found

Towards mid-morning, when the rain had thinned out into a drizzle, Sam caught sight of a human figure outlined against the sky on Rattle Tor. He and the two Narracott lads and their ponies were spread out in a line moving slowly across that part of the moor, keeping just within sight of each other. Visibility had lengthened to about a quarter of a mile and several tors had come into sight, including Raven's Tor which they had already searched. Sam sent out a big shout and changed course, knowing the Narracotts would copy him. He thought the figure might be Pa and he was right. The four of them came together just beneath the rocks of the tor.

Pa held a stick in his hand, which he held out for Sam's inspection.

'Have 'ee seen that afore somewheres?'

''Tis Peter's cow stick,' Sam said at once. 'I can mind how Granpa cut 'un for 'im out o' that cherry tree in garden.'

'So I thought,' said Pa. ''T was layin' over there in all that clitter under Rattle. Most like he had a tumble and took hurt an' so never thought to pick it up again when he went on.'

'We've found a clue then,' said the elder Narracott. 'This here's on the way to the Cleave.'

'Ay, the Cleave. I've bin figurin' it out thisways – he'd likely tend to keep his back to a tearing rain like we've had an' that would herd 'im towards the Cleave, where he'd find a bit o' shelter if nowt else. So you boys go on down to the river and do some callin' an' maybe I'll follow 'ee later.'

He wanted to go back first to the home moors, where most of the party from Martha Tavy were spun out in a long line, moving north. They were on foot, but there was a section of them on ponies still searching beyond Raven's Tor. He knew Ma and Beth were with them and he wanted to tell them he had found the stick and that the boys were going to the Cleave.

When he found them they looked so wet and dejected that he tried to persuade them to go home and leave the searching to people who were less tired. But having seen my cow-stick they wouldn't even consider such a thing, but wanted to stay with Pa and go into Tavy Cleave. Pa changed his mind then, however, because he had thought of another possibility. It stood to reason, he said, that now the rain was easing off Peter must be on the move *somewhere* and since he was not on any of the home moors he was most likely on his way down one of the streams. The Tavy was going to be searched by the boys, so that left the Walkham and the two that ran down into Martha. He persuaded Ma and Beth to go down one of the small streams and asked one of the men from the search party to go with them. Then he arranged for three others from the search party to undertake the second small stream, and set off himself for the Walkham valley. They all agreed before starting that they would go to the first house they came to in each of these three valleys, assuming that this was what I would do. In this way they hoped to avoid the long delay that would probably occur before any news of me could be carried to the villages from any one of these isolated farmhouses where I might arrive.

Now that he had a definite aim in his mind, Pa covered the ground at breakneck speed. The long slopes into the Walkham valley he descended at a steady run and was beside the rushing water in less than half-an-hour. In another fifteen minutes he was knocking on the door of the first farmhouse, where a woman was at work in the kitchen. She listened to his story with much sympathy, but had no news to give him. She did have a suggestion, however. Her husband worked at the Merrivale granite quarry, which was only a short way farther down the valley. There would be men there who would be glad to help in the search. He had only to ask the quarry manager and she was sure he would arrange it.

So Pa had to go on down and do the very thing he most hated to do – tell the story of his lost child to a whole crowd of tough quarrymen. The manager sent someone over to the Merrivale Inn five minutes away on the main Tavistock road to give the news there and soon another search party was setting out up the Walkham on the same route by which Pa had descended. But he was not among them, for he was already cutting across the shoulder of moors to the west of Merrivale in order to join the search in one of the streams running down to Martha Tavy. His energy and strength were still unabated, although he had had nothing to eat since four in the morning and only stream water to drink.

Meanwhile the three boys in Tavy Cleave had thought of a more practical idea for their search than anyone else on the moor that morning. It was the idea of Ted Narracott, the eldest. As soon as after much difficulty they had managed to get their ponies down to the river, Ted said he was going to look for footprints. As he pointed out, after a night of such rain it would be next door to impossible for anyone to walk down a valley like that and not leave very definite prints in all the soft places. He insisted on going first, on foot leading his pony, bending over and tracking like an American Indian.

When he found the first ones he called up Sam, made him dismount and try his foot in the print. All three boys saw at once that the boot which had made that print had been several sizes smaller than Sam's. Definitely then it must be mine, they said, for what other child in the whole wide world could possibly be walking down a wild place like Tavy Cleave alone after such weather as they had been having?

'We've found 'im,' Sam shouted in sudden delighted triumph. They had been calling my name at intervals for some time and now they gave a louder call in unison, then listened intently. But it was hard to make any sound prevail against the roaring of the water. This was getting gradually louder and would continue to do so all day as the river level rose. Although the rain had now stopped, Dartmoor was only just beginning to shed its new load of water.

They went on finding prints in good numbers all the way down the long winding valley. Ted, pretending to be a professional hunter, said they were so fresh they could not be more than half-an-hour old. But nevertheless when they came at last to a wall separating the wilds from rich green pastures they still had not seen a sign of me and from that wall onwards the grass was too long for any more prints.

A big house of grey stone soon confronted them, but Ted who knew the district said at once – ''Tis no good stoppin' here. No one'll live in this ole place, not since farmer Slocombe went crazy and killed his wife in it 'bout ten years agone.'

So they went on down the valley to a pretty white-washed farmhouse with a curl of smoke rising from a chimney, where they felt certain they would find me. But the woman in the kitchen only stared at them and listened to their story in amazement.

So they had to go on to the next house, and the next, spreading the story of me all down the road to Mary Tavy, but not hearing a word of news about me in return.

They began to think I must still be ahead of them, trying to walk home, for some reason too shy to call at any of the houses. Finally they reached the middle of Mary Tavy and stopped there, extremely puzzled and disappointed, wondering what to do next. The church clock said half-past-twelve and they were famished.

14. River Music

Next time I woke up it was broad daylight. It was still raining, but it was so wonderful to be able to see properly again that I didn't mind very much about the rain – at least, not until I had scrambled to my feet and gone out into it. Then I started to feel shivery at once, so I retreated and crouched down again under the rocks and bushes round my hole. I could see I was in a sort of ravine and I could hear the unmistakable roaring of a big stream of water not far away. That noise had not been there last night, so I knew it must have come because of the rain.

I had to think what to do. At first there seemed to be three possible things to choose from – to stay where I was until the rain stopped, to find the stream and follow it down until it reached fields and farms and houses, or, thirdly, to climb up again on to the open moor and have a good look round and recognize some landmarks like Raven's Tor and so make my way back to the moor-gate. It was terribly difficult to decide which to do. If I stayed where I was I would be wasting precious daylight and the rain might go on all day and then I would have to spend another night in the hole. That was really too horrible to face, for if I did that I could easily have another dream in which

I might meet Grark again, or worse still become a wolf myself and go howling across the moors in the wolf-pack and tear to pieces some poor sheep or dying pony. No, whatever happened I could not bear another night in the hole, not even if I slept all through it.

So that left two things to choose from, and I didn't much like either of them. What was wrong with going down the stream was, that I had no idea which stream it was likely to be and had no way of finding out. There were two big ones, the Tavy and the Walkham, the first leading down to Mary Tavy and the second to Merrivale which was miles away on the main road to Postbridge and Exeter. There were also two small ones leading down to Martha Tavy. If it was one of the small ones that I had below me then I was sure it would be best to follow it, for it couldn't be very far to go. But it was making such a roar and the ravine seemed so big and wide that I was pretty sure it was one of the big ones. If it was the Tavy then it would take me down through Tavy Cleave, one of the wildest and loneliest valleys of Dartmoor and a winding one too. Beth and I and Sam had sometimes looked down into it from above on some of our longer pony rides on lovely summer days and it had always looked frightening. Sam once wanted to go down into it, I remembered, but Beth and I refused because it looked too rocky and steep to take ponies into. It would certainly reach the green farmland of Mary Tavy in the end, but it would be an awfully long way to go and it would be leading away from Sunset instead of towards it. If it was the Walkham it would be smaller and shorter, but that also would lead away from Sunset and would end on a main road many miles from both the Tavy villages.

What was wrong with going up again on to the open moor was that it might prove to be not any part of the moor that I could recognize. If I could not recognize it, and if the rain made it impossible to see more than a short distance in front of me, then I might walk in circles again as I had last night. I might walk in circles all day and then at the end of it not even be able to find a badger's hole to creep into.

Then I started thinking about the family and what they might be doing to find me. It is an extraordinary thing that I should have thought first about how to rescue myself and only second about how other people were going to rescue me. It just shows how it is possible, however young you are, to grow up, or at least to grow about ten years older, in one day and a night. Because I had become an artist during the day and a farmer's boy during the evening and a wild animal during the night, I found myself the next morning making plans for rescuing myself more like a grown man than a child.

Of course it was also partly because I didn't believe that anyone, not even Pa, could possibly find me on those endless moors in pouring rain. I felt so small, so dwarfed by the great distances, as if I were a needle in a haystack. Also, it never entered my head that a properly organized search-party from the village would soon be out looking for me. I never thought I could be important enough for that. I pictured Pa and Ma and Sam and Beth doing all the searching and for just four people I really would be like a needle in a haystack. When I thought back to that long stretch of straight running that I had done in the last of the daylight, when I had kept the wind and rain behind me and gone on at a steady jog-trot uphill, then it seemed to me only too likely that I had gone right away from our home moors. I had hoped at the time to be going towards Raven's Tor, but if I really had been I could never have reached this place where I was now. There was no ravine like this and no big stream anywhere near Raven's Tor, of that I was certain. I must have been either too far to the left, which would be in the direction of Tavy Cleave, or too far to the right, which would be in the direction of the Walkham. So the more I thought about it the less likely it seemed to me that the family would ever find me.

All this time I was crouching at the entrance to the badger's set, where the overhang of rocks and bushes kept the rain off. I was stiff and cold and badly wanted to move about, to stretch and get warm. I was also hungrier than I had ever been in my life. Every now and then the sight and smell of bacon frying on our kitchen stove came drifting into my mind. I wondered too if that badger who had come sniffing at me in the night had found any food? And where was he likely to be at this moment, still out in the rain after his great fright, or would he have come back and got into his home by another entrance? I knew badgers' sets always had at least two entrances, sometimes three or four.

That started me thinking about tracks, for below me there was a bank of wet earth which would surely show marks of any animal setting foot on it. I was glad of this as an excuse for putting off a little longer any decision about which plan of action to choose. So I walked out on to the bank and took a careful look round in the rain, which seemed to be lessening a little. There certainly were fresh tracks, a lot of them, and criss-crossing, so that it looked rather as if two badgers might have come to smell at me in the night. It was pleasant to see this evidence of recent life. It made me feel less lonely. If I could have met a badger at that moment I would have spoken to him like a brother. I suppose it was around six o'clock by this time and I had not seen a human face nor heard a human voice for nearly ten hours. The lack of them had already made me different. I had taken on some of the endurance and independence of a wild animal.

Now that I was out in the rain I could see that what I had thought last night were trees were in fact only tall bushes growing amongst huge rocks. I could also get a glimpse now of foaming white water down below in the ravine. It certainly was a big stream, more like a river, and could easily be the Tavy. I could see, too, the way I had come down last night and it led up to a ridge which cut off the view completely. Above it the sky was full of racing grey clouds and there was something comforting about being able to see them, because it surely must mean that all the fog had gone and that the curtains of rain were getting thinner.

At last I decided what to do, although it was only half a decision. I would climb up to the top of the ridge to get a view of the moors and then, if there was nothing I could recognize, I would return the same way, get down to the river and follow the way it was going.

The climb warmed me up and made me feel much better. As I had hoped, there *was* quite a wide view from the top and two tors were visible, though neither of them looked at all like Raven's Tor. There were sheep and lambs scattered about and three or four ponies with their foals, but nothing else, no familiar landmarks at all. I looked very closely at each pony in turn, in case one might have a rider on it. Of course I listened very hard too, for it was obvious that if any of the family were searching they would also be calling – but there was nothing, only the wind and the rain and the soft roaring of the river in the ravine I had climbed out of. Lambs were calling and their mothers answering them now and then, and there were occasional croaks from ravens and mournful screams from buzzard hawks, but these sounds are really only part of the great Dartmoor silence.

It was not a very hopeful prospect. I had no idea at all which direction to take. The one safety rule that I had forgotten was the one about taking one's direction from the wind, but in this case it would not have helped me much for it almost certainly must have been blowing from the south-west up the Tavy or from the south up the Walkham.

I was wet through again by now and soon began getting cold as I stood still there in that horrible state of uncertainty. At last I turned round and went back. It would have been a right decision if I had had two good boots on my feet. I knew there was something wrong with one boot, but I had not sat down to examine it properly. I had not dared to do so.

It only took a few minutes to get back to my badgers' hole, but from there down to the river bed was such a rough scramble that just as I was reaching the bottom the sole of one of my boots tore away from its upper. I had to sit down and see just how bad the damage was. All the stitches round the front part of the boot had broken and only the heel was holding the sole in place. When I tried walking the sole flapped up and down and bits of my toes came through on to the ground. Then I looked at the other boot and saw that that showed signs of going the same way. They were old boots that Sam had outgrown. Naturally I wore my oldest boots for farm work.

I began to get frightened again then, the first time I had been frightened since waking up. This was going to slow me down terribly. If only I had some stout string I could more or less cure the trouble, but where would I find any string in this wilderness? Then I had an idea.

I was wearing braces to keep my trousers up. I took them off at once, bound them several times round the two gaping parts of the boot and then knotted them together. Then I got up and walked and found that it worked moderately well.

So I set off again, down-stream, holding my trousers up with one hand. The easiest place for walking was close to the water, where there were either grassy banks or pebbly beaches. But every now and then great jumbles of rocks jutted out into the river, completely blocking my way. Every time this happened I had to clamber from boulder to boulder across the river to get to more banks and beaches on the other side. It would have been fun if I hadn't been lost and alone, very hungry, rather frightened and walking lame. Sometimes I came to waterfalls, with deep rock-pools below them, the sort of places where you can have wonderful bathes in very hot weather. Whenever we did this, in those days, we used to feel very daring and wicked, because we had been taught that it was shameful to be naked.

The sound of rushing water filled my ears all the time and I got splashed a good deal too, though of course I hardly noticed it because I was wet through already. It was proper river-music and by the time I had been in that valley for an hour or two it had really worked its spell on me, like the sea does when you walk beside its breaking waves for a long time. I was walking in a sort of dream, with nothing more to worry about because the river was telling me I was coming down off the moors all the time and there were no more decisions to make. My boot was holding together just well enough to let me use that foot, but it made me very slow and my toes were rubbed raw.

How long I kept going in that strange sleep-walking fashion I had no idea at the time, but I can guess now that it must have been well over four hours, perhaps five. At the end of it, in rain so slight now that it was merely a drizzle, I came to a wall, the first man-made thing I had seen since the moor-gate, and when I climbed up on to the wall to get over it I found on the other side lush green grass and in the distance, beyond more walls and some big trees, was a house, a real house with chimneys and windows and real people inside it, or so I hoped. If I could I would have *run* across those lush green fields under those great comforting trees. But I was in a bad state by this time, unsteady on my feet, the toes of one foot bleeding, my clothes torn and muddy.

It was a large forbidding house of grey stone, with farm buildings round it. I walked right up to it, with my eyes fixed on its very odd-looking downstairs windows. Did they all have curtains or shutters drawn across them? When I was close enough I saw that they were boarded up – no glass, only boards of old wood nailed across them. It was like seeing a face with no eyes.

I was too tired to cry or make any sort of fuss in my mind. I just wanted to find some place to lie down and forget everything. So I went into the farm buildings, which mostly had doors open, found a heap of hay in a corner of one, threw myself down on it and went off to sleep in less than a minute.

When I woke up the first thing I noticed was watery sunshine coming in through a window. I jumped up quickly and saw something in the doorway which made me gasp for a moment. It was a huge tawny brown head with short straight horns and big dark eyes.

'Oh, hullo, cow,' I said, recovering at once from my fright. It was chewing the cud and watching me with a very placid but definite interest, as if glad to see something that relieved its boredom. But it was surely too big for a cow. I went up closer and bent down to look underneath it. Sure enough there was a bag hanging down between its hind legs, so it was a bull. That didn't frighten me, because

I was accustomed to our Sunset bull, who was usually as quiet as a cow. But it did mean that I would have to take care getting out of that building. He obviously had no intention of moving from there as long as he had me to watch. If I tried to slip past between him and the doorway he might give me a playful prod with one of those horns, each of which looked as massive as the horn of a blacksmith's anvil.

I noticed that the window, which was just a hole in the wall, was out of my reach. But there were three or four big drain pipes lying in a corner. I rolled one of these underneath the window and stood it up on end against the wall. With the help of this I climbed into the window hole easily enough and jumped down on to the grass outside. The bull never even moved, nor stopped cudding. I walked through the yard and out into an orchard, where there were several cows and calves. Then I climbed a gate and was in a grass-grown lane which I followed at a quickening pace, for I could already see another house in the distance. As I neared it this proved to be a white-faced friendly house with smoke rising from a chimney. I also heard a cock crowing and hens cackling, and then, wonderful and glorious, a woman singing.

I don't know what sort of woman she really was, nor do I remember her name. But I do remember that she looked nice, she felt nice and she smelled nice. She was out in the yard hanging up some washing and I ran and treated her as if she were Ma. I put my arms round her waist, hid my face against her dress and started to cry.

I don't think she said one word, she just picked me up and carried me indoors and sat down with me in a rocking chair. Then she rocked me and hugged me while I cried, for a long time.

15. The Cavalcade

It had been arranged that Martha Tavy post office was to be the headquarters of the search for me, the place where any news or suggestions or messages should be exchanged. So it was there, during the dinner hour, that a considerable crowd of people had assembled, amongst whom were Ma and Beth and also Pa, for by this time both the parties of three which had descended the two small streams had arrived in the village and Pa had come over from Merrivale to join one of them. They had called at a number of isolated farms but had achieved nothing except a wider spreading of the story.

The crowd was in a serious and anxious mood, though a good deal of animated discussion was going on. Offers of help of various kinds were coming in all the time, for example from Mrs Dodd who came over from the school and said she would arrange for a party of the older children to go out and help in the search that afternoon. The village innkeeper was there to say that his two-horse wagonette, which he used for taking people to and from Tavistock station, was standing in his yard at the service of anyone who needed it.

There was a convenient low wall in front of the post

office and upon this Ma and Beth were sitting, with other tired searchers, having food and drink brought out to them by sympathizers from the adjoining houses. As soon as she saw Mrs Dodd Ma asked her if Beth's special friend, Maisie, was in school that day and if so, could she come and keep Beth company? This was readily agreed to and made all the difference to Beth, who had for some time been perilously close to tears. She was able to pour out the whole story to Maisie while Ma and Pa were busy taking part in the discussion about what to do next. There was general agreement that everything depended now upon Sam and the Narracott lads. If they too had drawn a blank, then the situation was indeed grave.

At one moment great interest was aroused by Miss Scrimshaw's brougham, a closed one-horse carriage, halting outside the post office, driven by her groom and with her visible inside it. She poked her head out of the window and called someone up to give her the latest news and to receive a parcel from her hands. This parcel was taken to the Vardens and proved to have 'For Peter Varden' written across it.

The person who brought to this crowd its first relief from seriousness and anxiety was a young man on the staff of the Tavistock weekly newspaper. He had been in Mary Tavy all the morning collecting facts about the mining accident, but just as soon as his nose for news got a whiff of this other story he had switched all his attention from the mine to the moor, from men to the boy. Mine accidents happened somewhere every year, but a young child lost on Dartmoor happened perhaps only once in a hundred years.

He was a confident handsome chap, well dressed and very well mounted. From the back of the crowd he was heard asking for Mr and Mrs Varden and for someone to hold his horse. When he was brought up to my parents he doffed his hat in style and bowed politely, even though they must have been looking their very worst after the sort of morning they had had. He looked and spoke mainly at Ma.

'Good day to you, Mam. I am addressing you on behalf of my newspaper, the *Tavistock Journal*. If you will give me a little information about this sad occurrence I believe I can be of assistance to you.'

Neither of my parents knew anything about the subtle ways and wiles of newspaper men. When he brought out his notebook and pencil they felt pleased and flattered by the idea of having anything they said put in the newspaper. They gave him the rough outline of the story and then answered his many questions quite freely until this seemed to be going on rather long. Pa said abruptly –

'Now, what about this help you mentioned, eh, Mister?'

'I'm coming to that,' the man said easily, then turned back to Ma. 'I take it, then, Mam, that this nine-year-old child of yours had already done a whole day's work on the farm?'

Pa was not accustomed to being ignored. He stepped forward in front of his wife, growling –

'I'll trouble 'ee to come to the point Mister.'

The younger man had to give way, especially as there were voices raised among the crowd in support of Pa.

'Very well sir, the point is this, and you no doubt will be able to judge better than I whether 'tis fact or fiction, I heard in Mary Tavy that three boys on ponies had come down through Tavy Cleave and had seen your boy's footprints all the way down.'

Ma and Beth both jumped up from the wall, Pa let out an oath and his eyes blazed.

'Why in thunder couldn't 'ee tell us that long since, yer

zilly gabbin' vool, 'tis the one bit o' news we've all bin waitin' for this last hour.'

In the commotion and excitement that followed, the newspaper man faded into the background. The first thing done was a message sent to the innkeeper asking for his wagonette and until it came Beth was dancing for joy and steps were being taken to get other carts and traps ready for the two mile trip to Mary Tavy. In the end it was an imposing cavalcade that trotted off, led by the two horse wagonette with about a dozen people on board, including of course the three Vardens and Maisie. Behind came pony-traps and milk-floats and riders of all kinds, followed by people on foot. The sun was shining now and there was much turmoil and excited shouting voices. A disaster was showing its first signs of turning into a festival.

About a mile out of the village a fantastic meeting took place. The wagonette had to slow to a walk because another though smaller cavalcade was seen approaching at speed, led by three boys riding abreast like the outriders of some important person's coach. Behind them were two pony-traps and a cart, all well filled with people.

The road became a jumble of restive horses being shouted at to keep still, but one shout made its meaning plainly heard above all the confusion –

'He's found – Peter Varden's found!'

16. Sunset at Sunset Farm

Aunt Alice was rather too much of a good thing. That is one of my clearest memories of that closing part of the adventure. She had never had children of her own, which perhaps was why she was not very good at handling them. She fussed over me as if I were about four years old and wouldn't let me sit on the seat beside her in the pony-trap, she made me sit on her lap which smelled of lavender that had somehow gone wrong. She had a shawl too that she kept trying to wrap round me and that smelled of mothballs. I was already wearing an old jacket that had been put on me at the farm, so the shawl was just a nuisance.

That unknown woman at the farm, who had rocked me and fed me and then put me in her own bed, she was a different matter altogether. I hadn't minded being made a fuss of by her because she didn't talk and smile all the time as Aunt Alice did. The farm woman was deep and quiet and had a voice that lingered over her words, the few that she did say. It was a voice that sang even when she wasn't singing. Aunt Alice was a dear kind person, I'm sure, but she seemed to me a bit silly with her incessant chatter and I was afraid she would make me look silly too.

I have to explain how she came into the picture at all.

You remember how Sam and the Narracott lads arrived in the centre of Mary Tavy village just at dinner time, feeling very downcast because after all they hadn't found me and had had nothing to eat since dawn? Well, naturally they decided to go to relatives. It was usual in those days for one's relatives to live in the villages round about. Sam suddenly realised that a Varden aunt lived in the main street. In a quarter of an hour the three boys were sitting at table eating a hearty meal and at the same time telling their story to a group of very interested people. That meant that the next stage in the rescue operation was taken out of their hands.

Our aunt was a leading resident of the village and had her finger in every pie. By the time they had finished their meal a horse and trap were ready outside the house, to take a search-party back to the farmhouses the boys had already visited. For there was general agreement that I must be still in that area somewhere, for I would have been noticed long since if I had walked on down into the village.

The three boys followed the trap on their ponies. About a mile uphill out of the village they all heard a clatter of hooves telling of someone approaching at speed. A horseman came swerving round a bend and pulled his horse up abruptly as soon as he saw what he was meeting. But he ignored the halted trap and came on alongside the boys.

'Be you the lads that called in to my place a while since? We've got 'im, that little 'un ye was hunting for!'

He seemed as highly pleased as if I were one of his own family. He went on to relate how when he had come in for his dinner his wife had sent him straight out again to try to catch the three boys on ponies. For by that time I had been in his house half-an-hour and had been fed and washed and put to bed, but his wife hadn't been able to go running out herself to spread the news. When asked by our aunt in the trap what sort of state I was in, the man replied that his wife had seemed happy enough about that and had said I was 'a proper picture of a boy and sleepin' like a babe'.

So that was how I came to be driving with Aunt Alice from Mary Tavy to Martha Tavy only an hour or so after I had been put to bed in the white-washed farmhouse. According to what Sam told me, the farm woman had not at all wanted to have me woken up and had made rather a scene about it on the doorstep, almost refusing to let Aunt Alice into her house. But Aunt Alice had her way. She said it wouldn't be fair to keep me hidden away there when there was such a hue and cry about me all through the countryside and my parents must be getting desperate.

I expected to have to sit there on her lap all the way home, so you can imagine how delighted I was when we met that wagonette at the head of its cavalcade and I suddenly realised that it was all something to do with me and that those three people standing up waving madly in the front seats were my parents and Beth.

As they started climbing down from the wagonette I wriggled quickly out of Aunt Alice's arms and jumped down into the road beside them. Ma and Pa each picked me up and gave me a hug in turn, then Beth caught hold of my hand and started swinging my arm, which was one of our special games. I could see she was all heaving inside, trying not to cry. She just managed not to and burst out laughing instead, though it was an awfully queer sort of laugh.

'Oh, just look at his *boots*!' said Maisie who had come up behind Beth and was looking at me as if she had never seen me before.

Pa had to discuss things with the coachman of the wagonette. I could tell from Ma's face that she had already taken in all that was wrong with my boots and clothes and was horrified and perhaps a little ashamed in front of all those people. She had to talk to Aunt Alice for a while but then decided that the best place for us was back on the wagonette so we three got up there and stayed talking and cuddling while Aunt Alice talked from below and the drivers of all the various traps and carts sorted out the muddle.

The wagonette had to be turned round, which meant driving on to find a wide place. When that was done we trotted back to Martha Tavy, with Sam and the Narracott lads as outriders again, Sam turning sideways on his pony every now and then to grin and wave at me. All the other people got off at the post office, but the wagonette drove on with us uphill towards Sunset, mainly to take us home, but partly also to bring down some of the people of the search parties. I hardly noticed what was happening because I had so much to talk about to Ma and Beth, between whom I was sitting.

There was only just room for that wagonette in our narrow lane. Nothing as big had ever been up it before, I believe, and the coachman was worried about ever being able to turn round.

The moors above Sunset were in sunshine as we ascended the last hill. We stopped talking to gaze up there, thinking of all that Dartmoor had done to us in the last eighteen hours. The tors were looking down at us, crystal clear and much closer than usual, as they had been early yesterday morning. Even Raven's Tor, the biggest one a long way off on the really high moors, showed all its jagged rocks clearly.

'I'll have to go up there on Jamey, soon as we get home, to call off the searchin',' Pa said, and he didn't say it as a grumble but almost as if he relished it. That was usually how it was with people like us living on Dartmoor's skirts.

If we hated the moors one day we would probably love them the next, and vice versa.

Pa was in a good humour at last. He turned to me –

'Think o' that, Peter boy – there's folk still looking for 'ee up there. An' if old Dartmoor had a mind to start another fog now, there'll be half a dozen of 'em lost in no time.'

I was impressed though I could tell that he was joking.

'How are you going to gather 'em, John, that's what I'm wondering,' said Ma.

'I'll try whistlin' for 'em,' said Pa. 'That powerful old whistle we used for trainin' the dogs. I reckon that'll gather 'em.'

When we drove into the farmyard, the three ponies leading and the wagonette rattling its four iron-shod wheels and its eight horse shoes on the cobbles with a noise to wake the dead, the grandparents were standing at the house door with open mouths.

I felt as if I had been away for a week. Pa carried me indoors and there Granma took a close look at me, but thank goodness did not fuss over me or ask me any questions. I was put in Pa's big chair by the kitchen fire while the grandparents were told the story. Then soon afterwards I must have been taken upstairs, because the next thing I remember is waking up in my bed, thinking it was morning, wondering where Sam was and why his bed had not been slept in. There were noises and voices below, so I dressed quickly and went down to find them all just about to start a meal, which I thought would be breakfast. How they all laughed when I asked for my porridge.

'Look at the clock, Peter!' they said, but when I did it said half-past-six, so I looked as blank as ever. They laughed louder and Ma said –

'The clock can't tell im whether 'tis morning or evening, how could it – 'tis us that's silly to think it could.'

Well, it was tea they were sitting down to and I had slept only three hours. In the middle of tea Ma jumped to her feet suddenly and said –

'Oh my dear lord I forgot Miss Scrimshaw's parcel – I left it under the seat in the wagonette an' 'tis surely gone back to village –'

'No 'taint,' Pa said. 'Sit down, me dear, 'tis in the front porch, coachman found it just afore he drove out an' I've only this minute thought of it myself. Beth can fetch it –'

She was already out of the room after it. It was a bulky heavy parcel with my name on it in Miss Scrimshaw's special kind of handwriting. They all watched as I undid the string. (We never cut string if we could help it, it was too precious.) Inside was a set of water-colour paints, several brushes, a palette and two large drawing-pads. There was also a note, which I asked Ma to read out. It said that these things were not new but had come from her own store of painting materials and that she was sure that I would make good use of them.

Beth was let off all work that evening. So was I of course, but that had been taken for granted without being mentioned. We were allowed to go in the parlour and play with this wonderful present, while everyone else was busy catching up with the farm and dairy work.

There were heavy showers of rain after tea. It was like a wet Sunday afternoon for me and Beth sitting there in the parlour at a table near the window, both painting, in a very quiet house, for even Granma was mostly in the dairy separating milk and doing preparations for butter-making.

At first we just played and talked, using the paints for pictures out of our heads on the drawing-pads, one of which I had given to Beth. Later we had to keep looking out of the window because things were happening in the sky. It had stopped raining and there was the beginning of the kind of sunset that you keep thinking of for days afterwards and that you remember in future whenever the word sunset is mentioned.

There was a bank of very dark rain-cloud edged with gold along the whole western horizon and out of it in two places massive great thunder clouds had reared up almost to the top of the sky. They too were edged with gold and flecked with unusual bronze and amber tints. They had thin streamers of cloud attached to them, like hair blowing out in the wind from giant heads. One of them gradually took the shape of an anvil while we watched. Overhead the sky was still light blue, though fading. All the low country towards Tavistock was a very dark purple-blue, Brent Tor with its church on the top standing out black, like a silhouette.

'I'm going to paint *that,* Beth,' I said suddenly. 'I'm going to watch everythin' goin' on out there and make it go on *here.*' I turned over a new sheet of paper on the pad and jabbed my finger down on it.

Beth would not paint any more after that, but simply sat watching, moving her eyes backwards and forwards between my drawing-pad and the sky. I was getting on well, while the sunset light was becoming even more wondrous, when Ma came hurrying in to say that we must go to bed. I implored her for a little longer time, saying that I was just in the right mood for *real* painting and that if I couldn't do this picture tonight I never would be able to do it at all, because in the morning all the magic would be gone.

She came to see what I had done, while I watched her face.

Then she turned back to the window and the western sky, with a look in her eyes that I had never seen before. They seemed to be looking far forwards in time. Sunset lights were playing on her face, too – gold and orange and purple and brown, making it no longer tired and worn but strangely beautiful.

We both waited for her to say something. It was a long moment, like time standing still. With a slow smile she said –

'Oh, Peter, what a *long* way away you've been. And you're hardly quite back with us even yet, are you?' Then she turned and walked quickly out of the room.

I have always remembered her words. They were her way of telling me that she understood what my longest day had done for me. I think in some deep part of her mind she was watching the misty moving shadows that the future is always throwing upon the present.

I only had until dark, which was about another twenty minutes. But the picture painted itself. I only had to do what something inside me told me to do. Those two thunder clouds came alive and fairly burned with the glory that the last rays of the sun were giving them, very high up and far away, long after all the lower cloud ranges had sunk nearly into night.

I still have that picture stored away somewhere in my house. It is so faded now, and so childish in form, that it cannot mean much to anyone but me. The only other person for whom it once had a meaning has been dead these last forty years. I showed it to her of course when I was taken to see her to thank her for her present. She looked at it for a good long time and then asked me to let her write something along the bottom. Her writing is still there, faint but legible. It says –

Sunset from Sunset Farm
Peter Varden, July 1880

ALEC LEA writes:

After some early years of wandering in Canada, New Zealand and Tahiti, I took up dairy farming in 1936 and stuck to it for 35 years, mostly in Devon. During the whole of that time I wrote adult fiction without much success except for three novels published in the 1940s. Persuaded by my wife to write a book for children, I wrote *To Sunset and Beyond* in six weeks. I have now given up farming and have moved with my family to Scotland, where I hope to write more books for children. My wife is a lecturer at Aberdeen College of Education.

An amateur film was made from the book, which has won most of the prizes and awards available for amateur films. The two main characters in it were played by my two children who were then 11 and 9.

If you have enjoyed this book and would like to know about others which we publish, why not join the Puffin Club? You will receive the club Magazine, *Puffin Post*, four times a year and a smart badge and membership book. You will also be able to enter all the competitions. For details send a stamped addressed envelope to:

The Puffin Club, Dept. A
Penguin Books Limited
Bath Road
Harmondsworth
Middlesex